GRADE-2 GEOMETRY AND MEASUREMENT

Fun-filled Activities

Identifying Plane Shapes

Identify each shape. Then write its name matching its number in the table below.

3-	4-	5-	6-
7-	8-	9-	10-

Quadrilaterals

A quadrilateral is a closed figure with four sides and four angles.

They can be grouped by sides, angles, length and parallel sides.

Cross out the shapes that are not quadrilaterals. Then write the correct name for each quadrilateral.

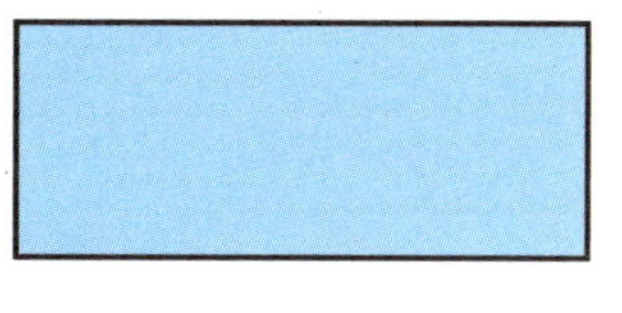 ____________

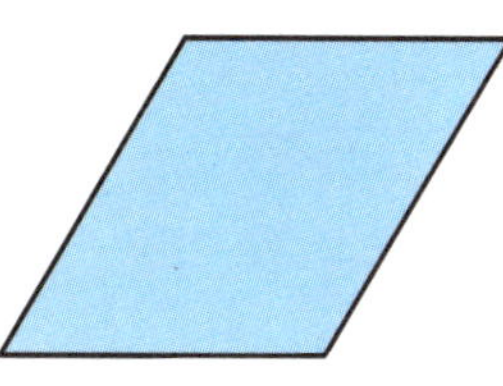 ____________

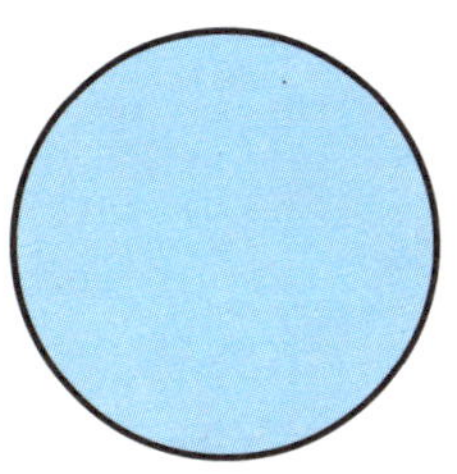 ____________

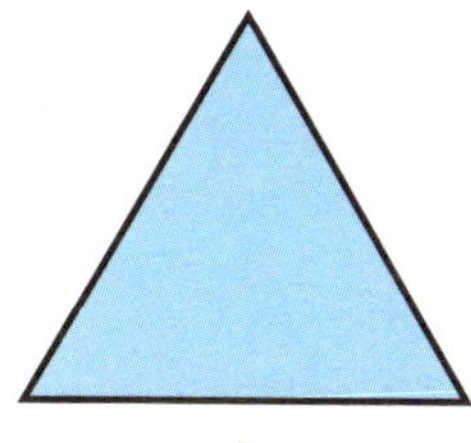 ____________

 ____________

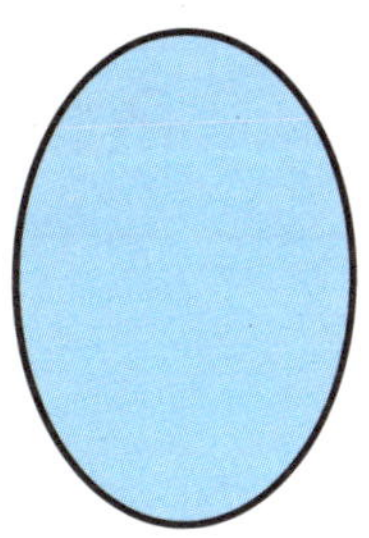 ____________

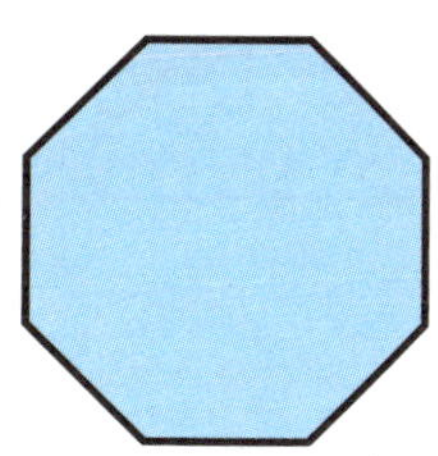 ____________

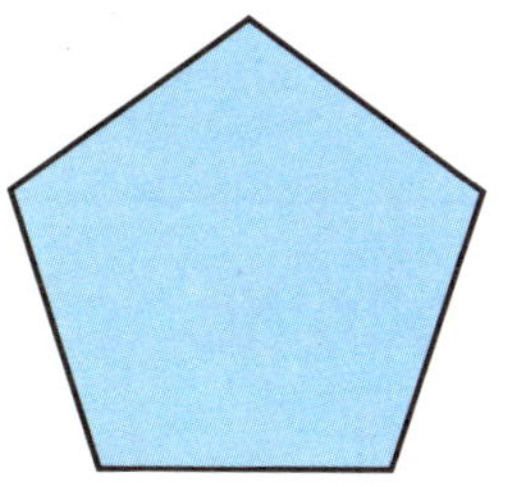 ____________

CHALLENGE

Fill in the table to compare the quadrilaterals.

Figure	Number of sides	Parallel sides	Angles
Square	4 equal sides	2 pairs of parallel sides	4 right angles

Properties Of Quadrilaterals

Read each definition below. Inside each quadrilateral, write the number of the definition that matches it.

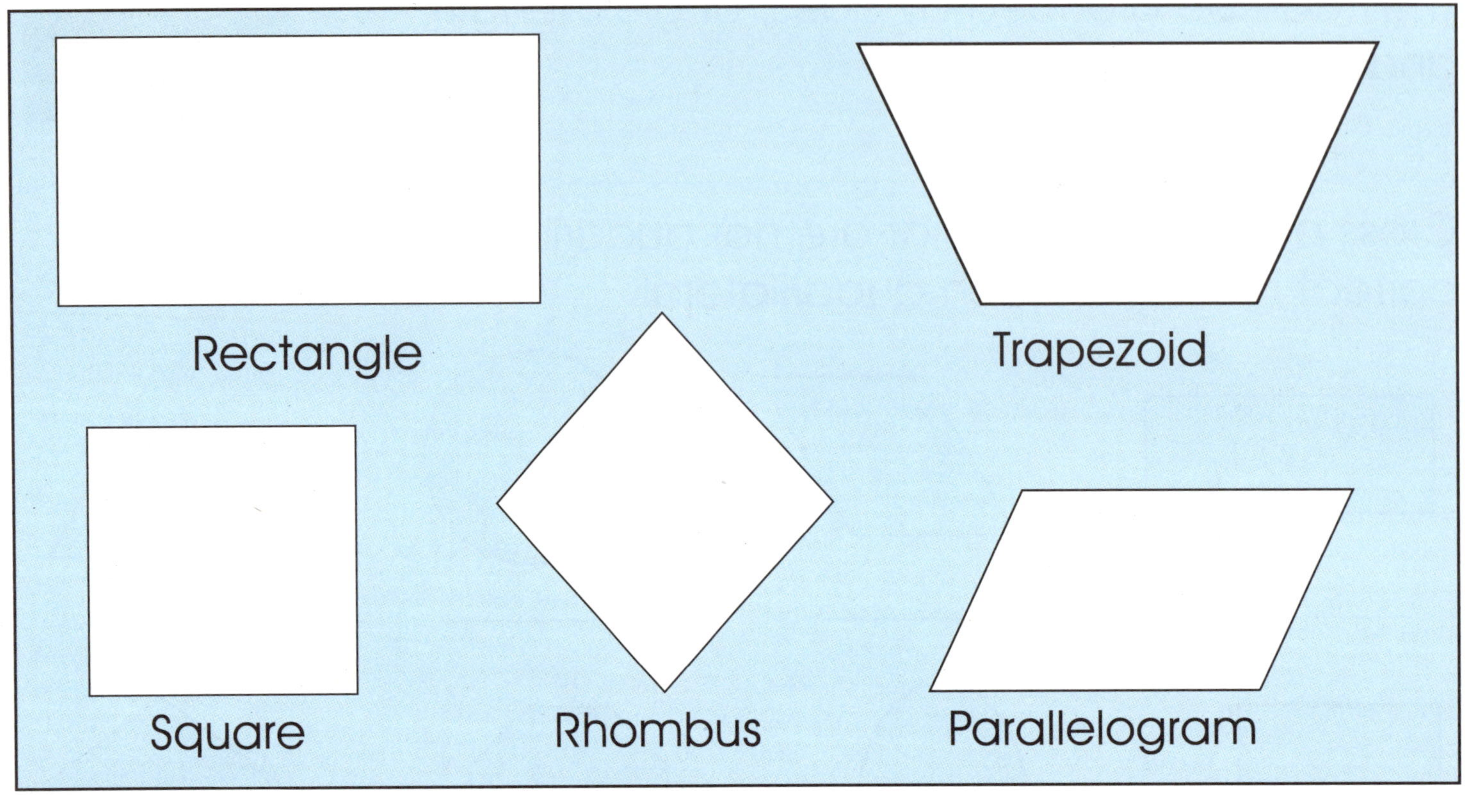

Definitions

1. a four-sided figure with all sides equal
2. a four-sided figure with opposite sides equal and parallel
3. a four-sided figure with only one set of parallel sides
4. a figure with all angles equal to 90° and all sides equal
5. a figure with opposite sides parallel but angles may vary

CHALLENGE

Tick the statements that are true.

1. A parallelogram is a kind of rectangle.
2. A square and rhombus are similar.
3. A rhombus is similar to a parallelogram.

Congruent Figures

Two figures are congruent if they are exactly the same shape and size. Their corresponding sides and angles are equal.

In each row, tick the shape that is congruent to the first one.

1. a. b.  c. 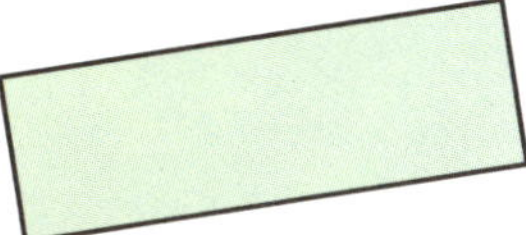

2.  a. 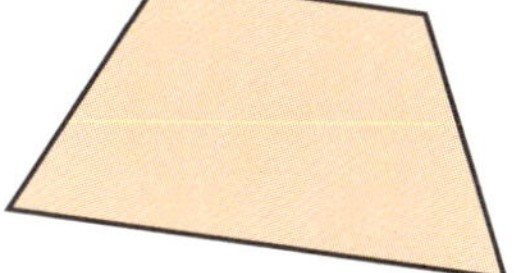 b. 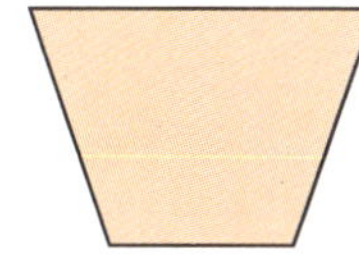 c. 

3. 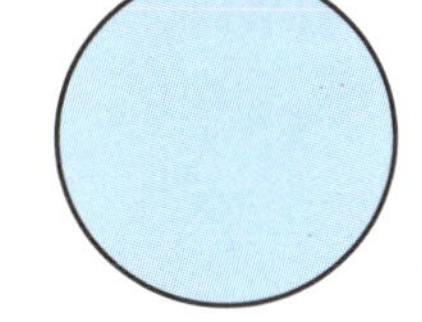 a.  b.  c. 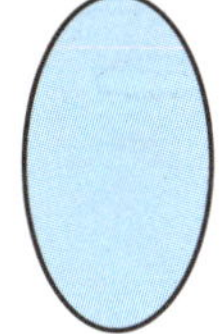

4.  a.  b. 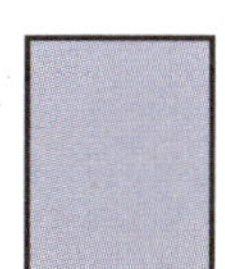 c. 

5. 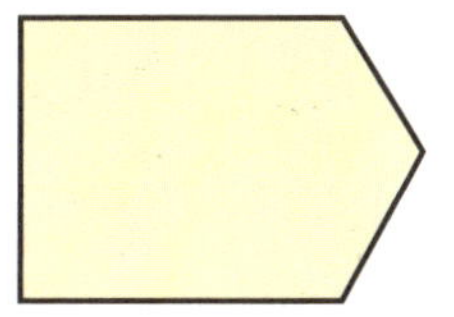 a. 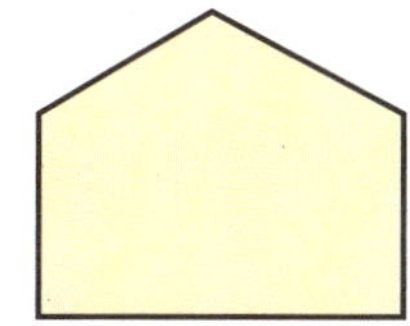 b. 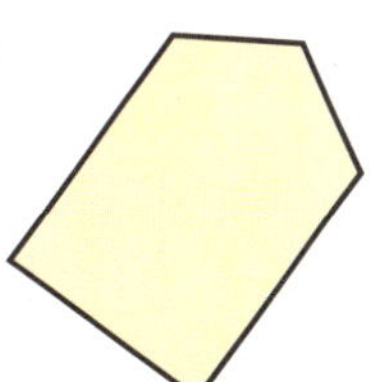 c. 

QUICK TIP

Congruent shapes may appear different because one is shifted or rotated a certain way, but they're still the same shape. All the sides of one shape are the same length as the corresponding sides of the other.

Congruent Figures

Identify the congruent figures for each shape from the picture given below. Write the matching letters.
Not all shapes may have congruent pairs.

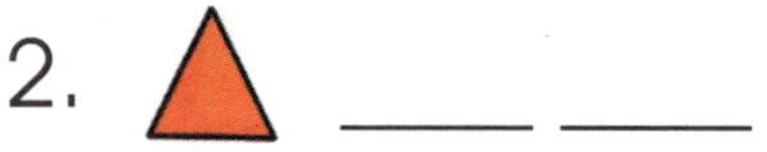

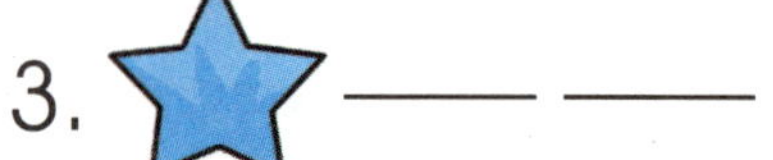

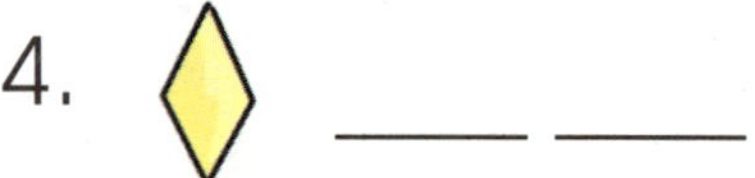

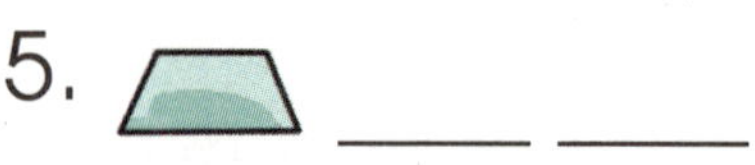

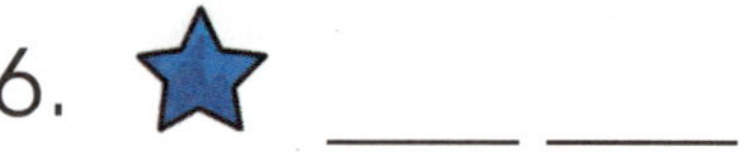

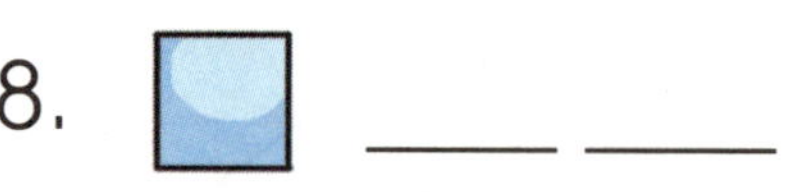

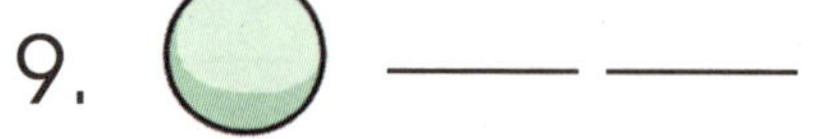

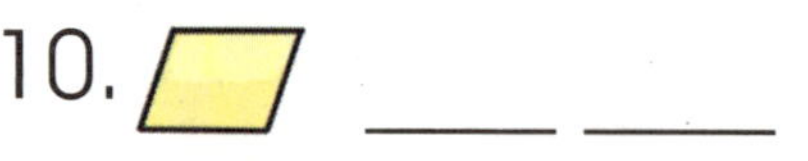

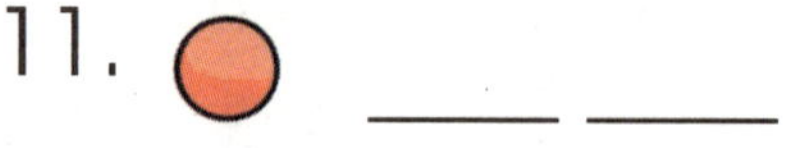

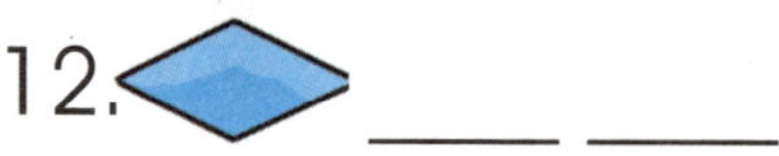

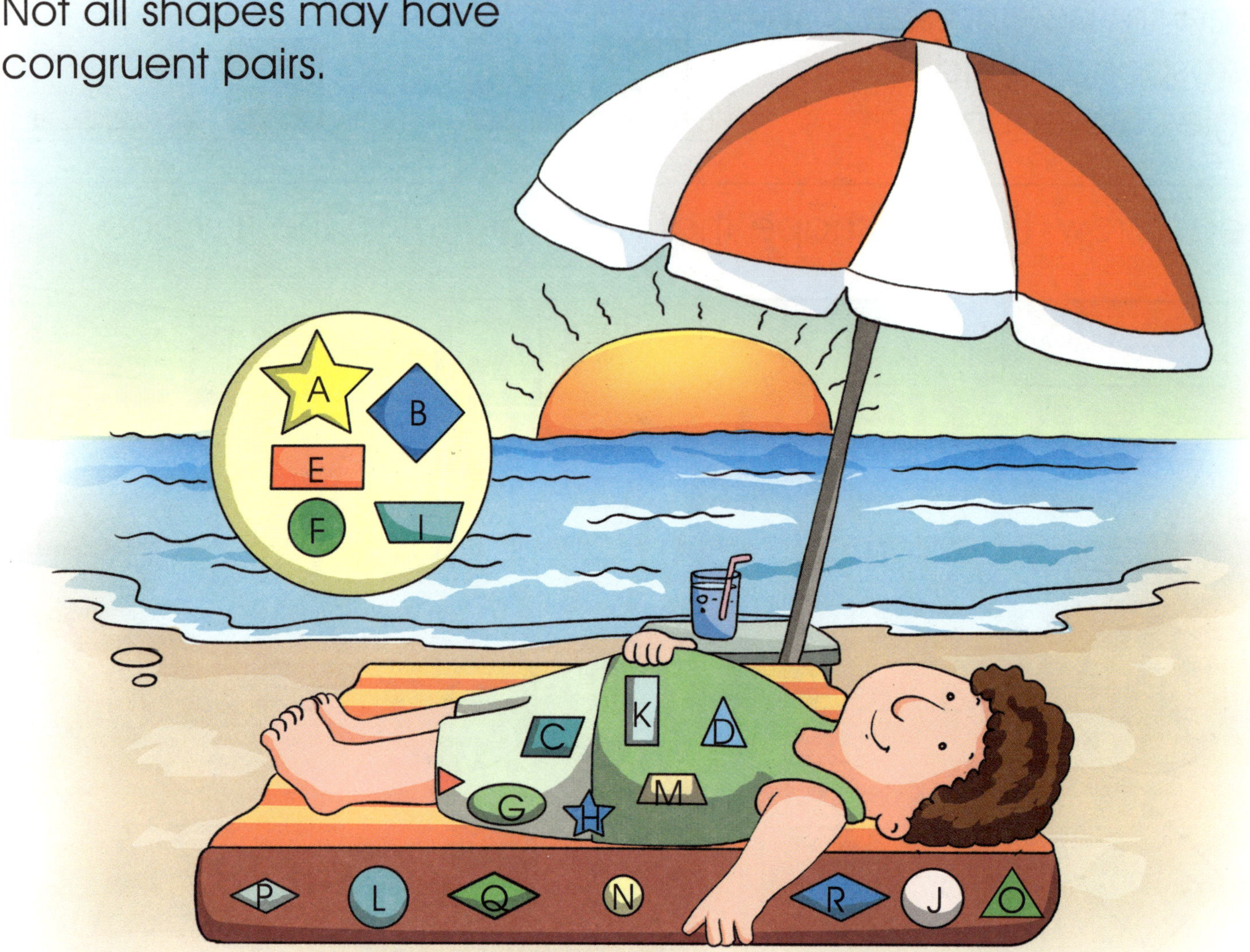

1. ____ ____
2. ____ ____
3. ____ ____
4. ____ ____
5. ____ ____
6. ____ ____
7. ____ ____
8. ____ ____
9. ____ ____
10. ____ ____
11. ____ ____
12. ____ ____

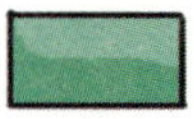

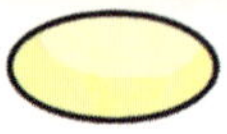

CHALLENGE

Why are these pairs not congruent? Explain.

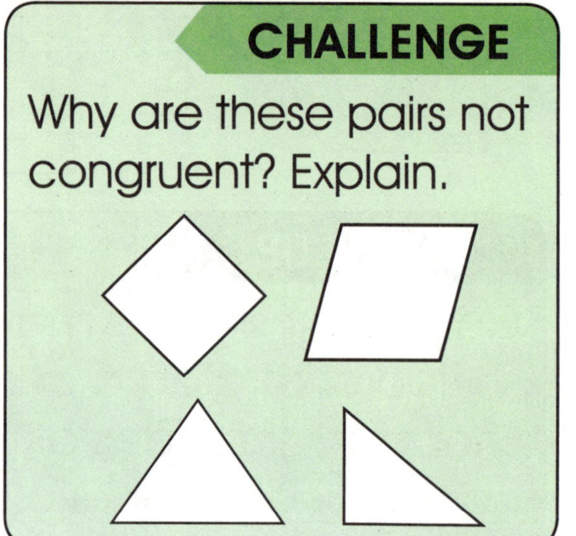

Congruent Shapes

Use a pencil and a ruler to draw a congruent shape for each figure on the grid. Colour when you draw.

A.

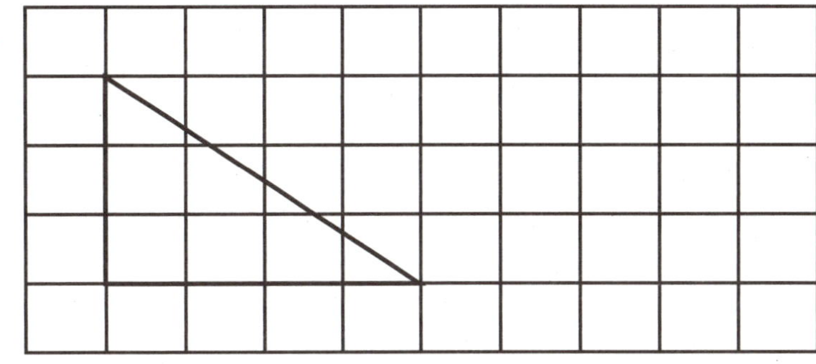

B.

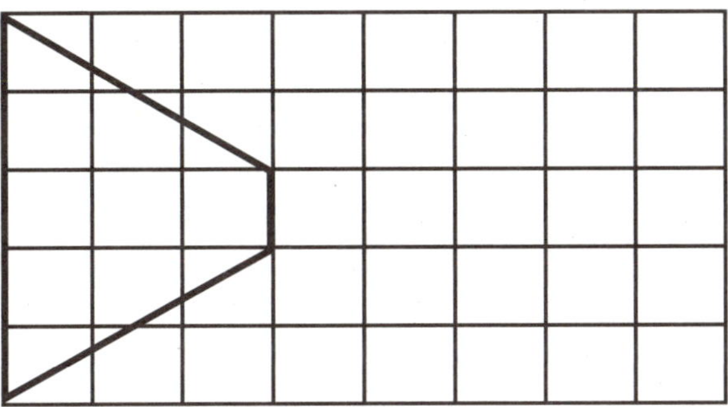

C.

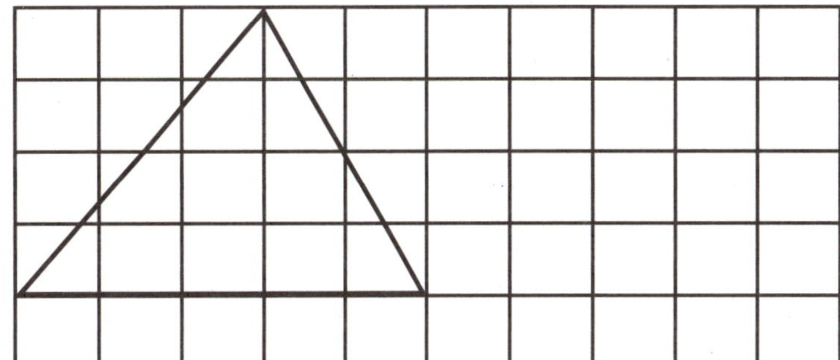

D.

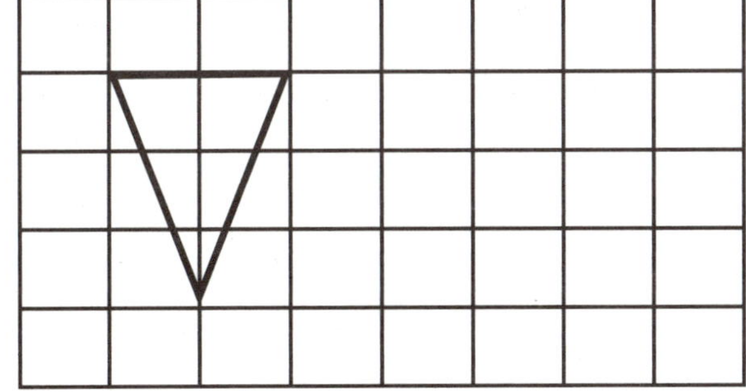

E.

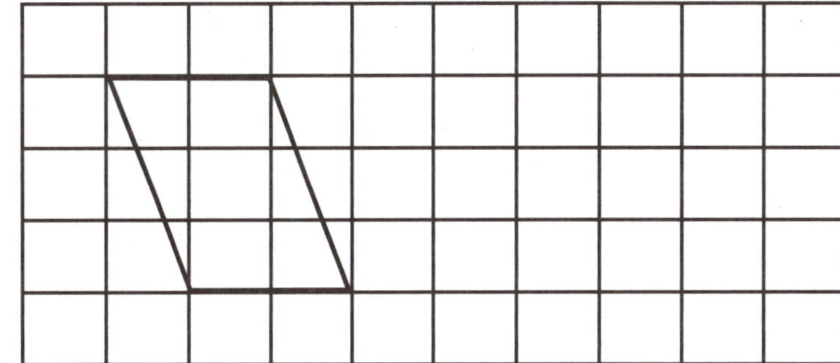

F.

G.

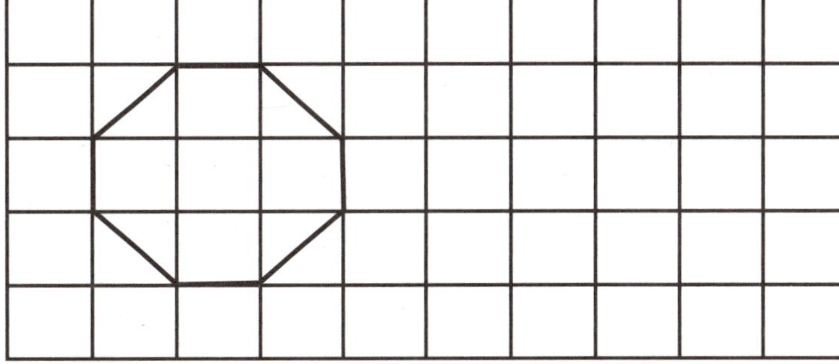

Solid Shapes

Tick the solid shape that matches each statement.

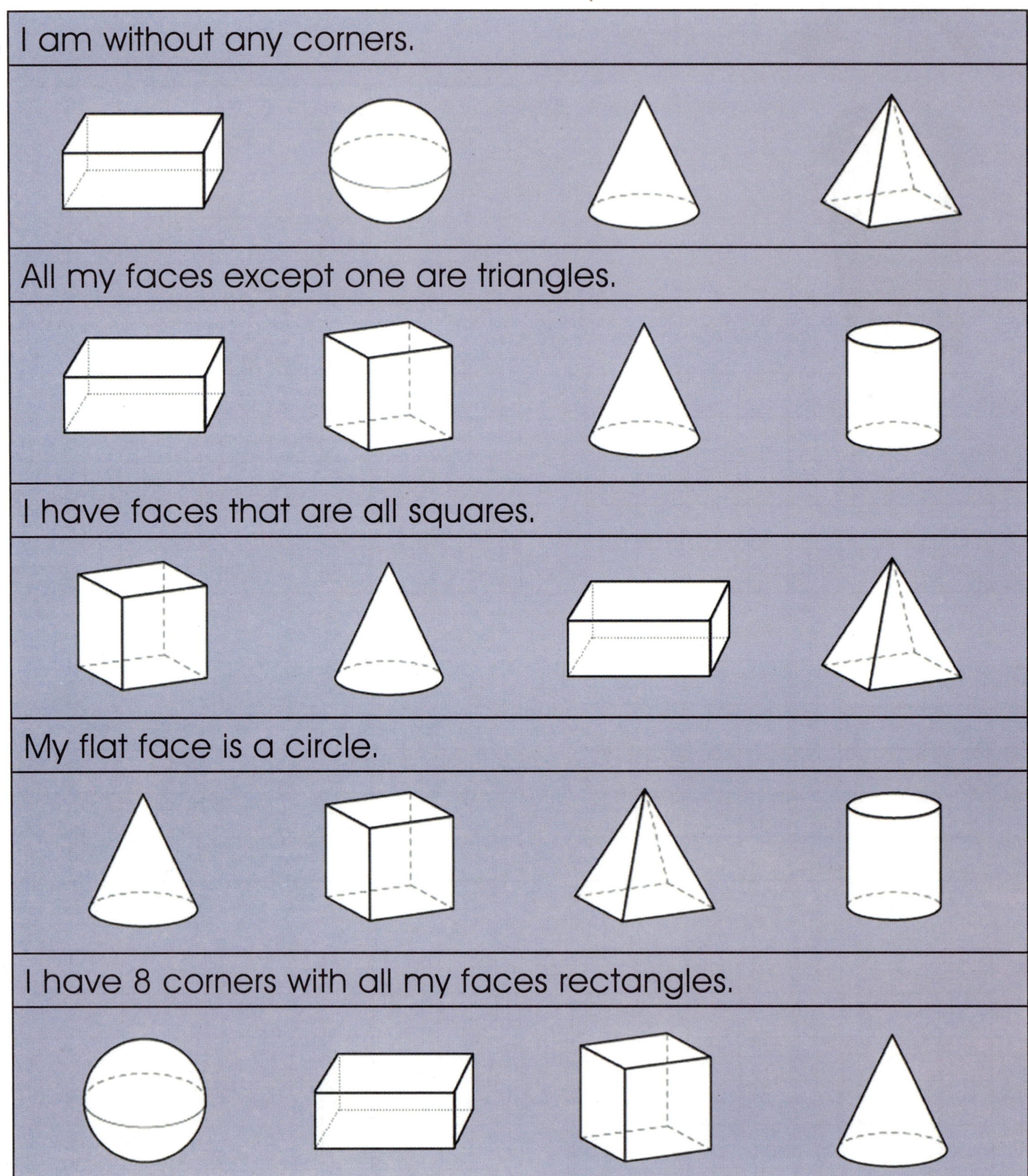

Solid Figures

Look at each model. Write the shape of each model and complete the table.

1. 

2. 

3.

4.

5. 

6. 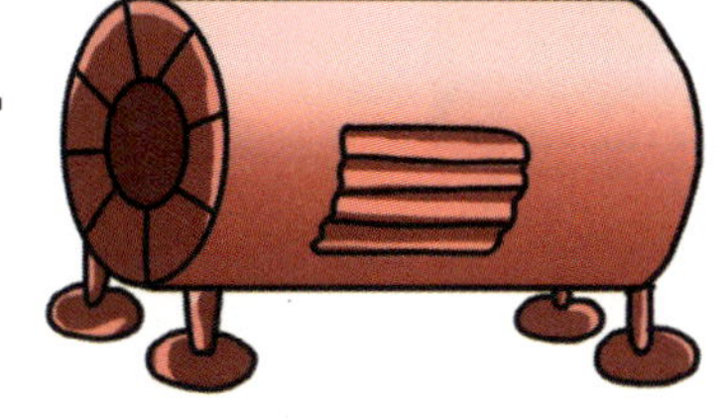

Shape of the model	Number of faces	Number of edges	Number of corners
1.			
2.			
3.			
4.			
5.			
6.			

CHALLENGE

Each model is made up of 2 solid shapes. Identify and name them.

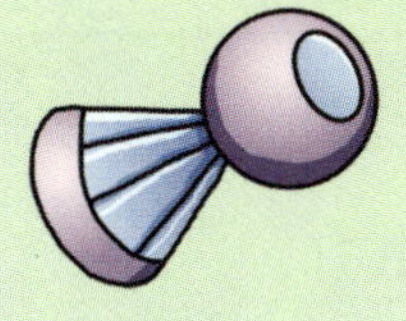
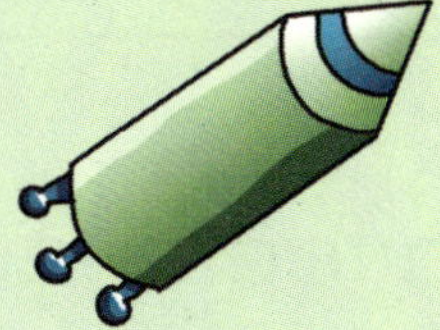
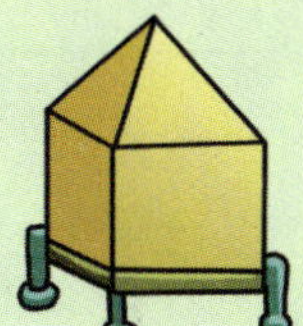

Word bank

Cone
Pyramid
Sphere
Cylinder
Cube
Rectangular prism

Solid Shapes

Each side of a solid figure is a face. For example:

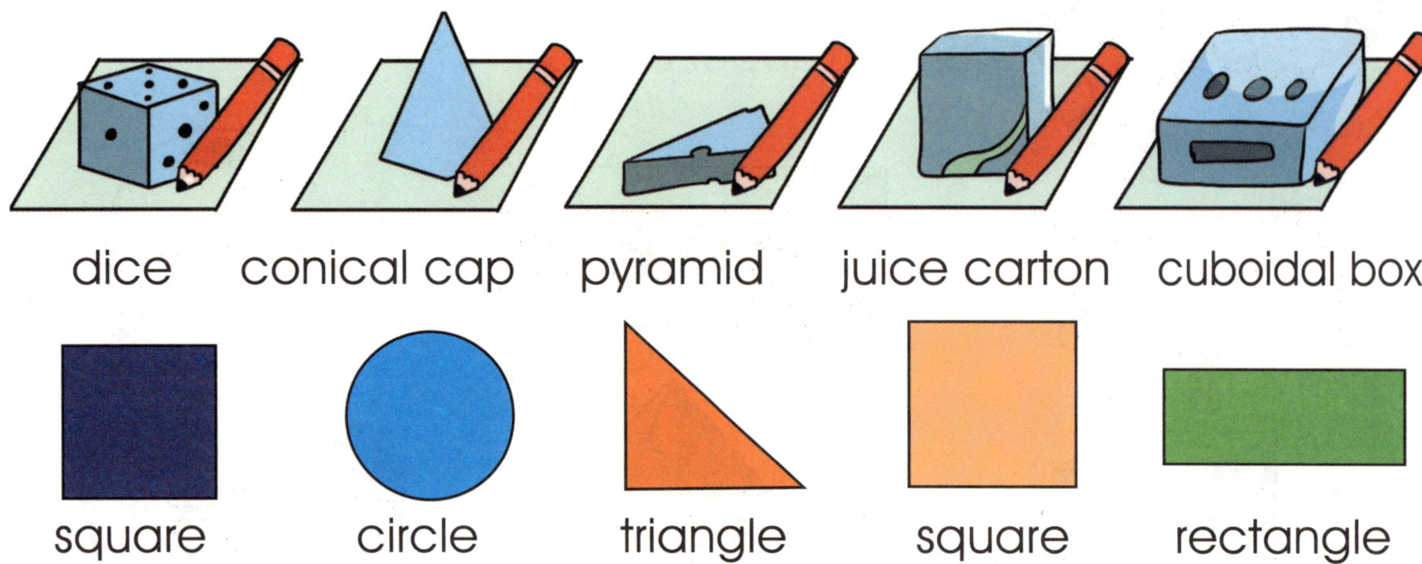

dice	conical cap	pyramid	juice carton	cuboidal box
square	circle	triangle	square	rectangle

Shape	Total number of sides	Plane figures			
		0	2	0	4

CHALLENGE

Draw the top view of a cube, a cone and a rectangular prism. How do they look like?

Attributes of Solid Figures

Which shape would you add to each shape below to form a new shape? Draw it.

+ =

− =

+ =

− =

− =

+ =

− =

Hints

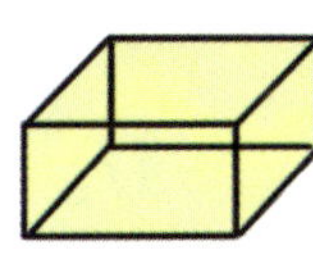
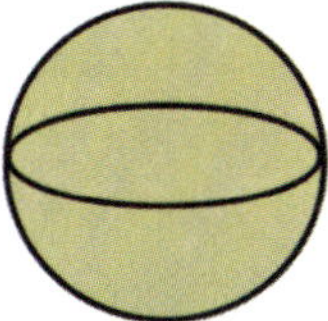
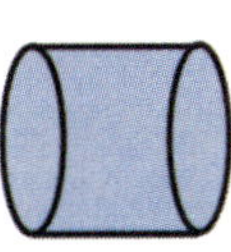

CHALLENGE

How would the number of faces and edges change when you join two cubes side by side?

Flip, Turn and Slide

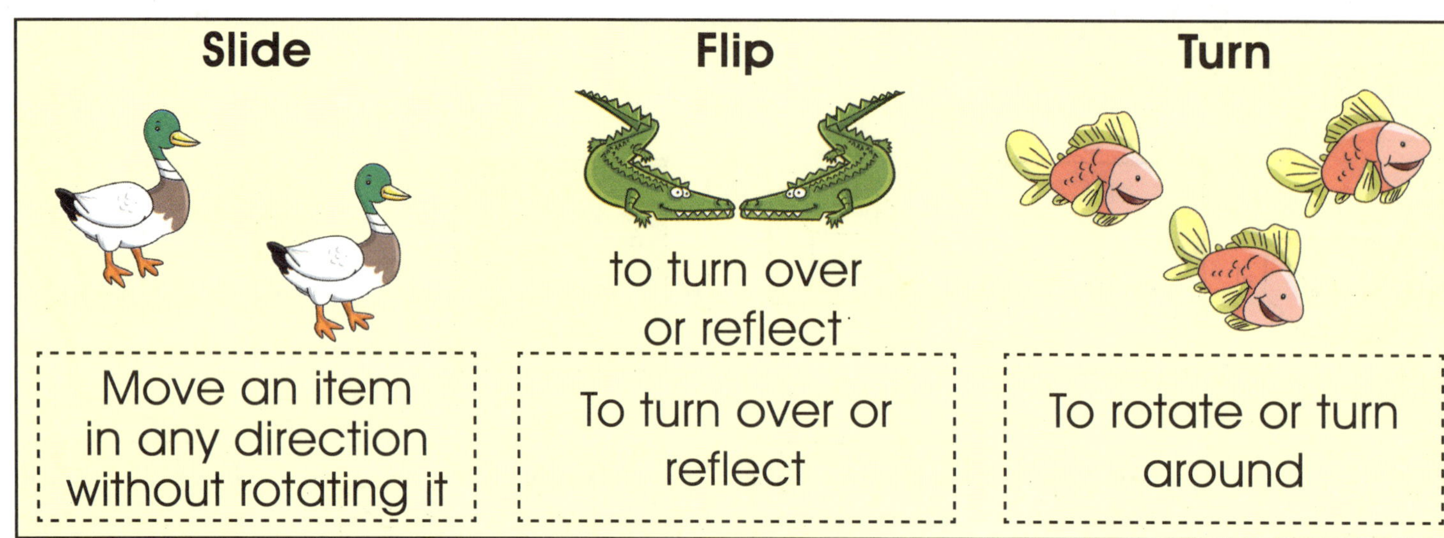

Write flip, slide or turn for each.

1.

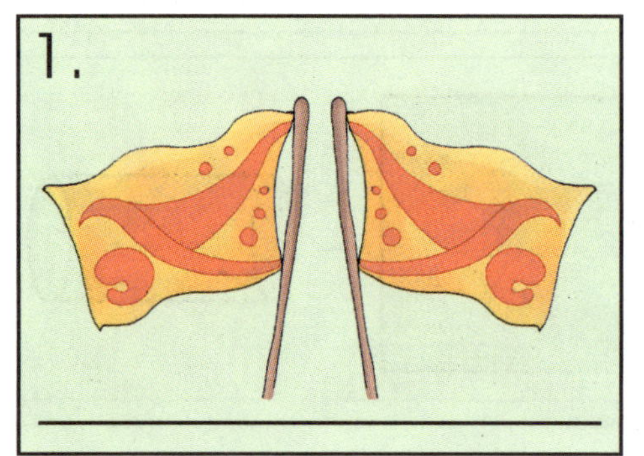

2.

3.

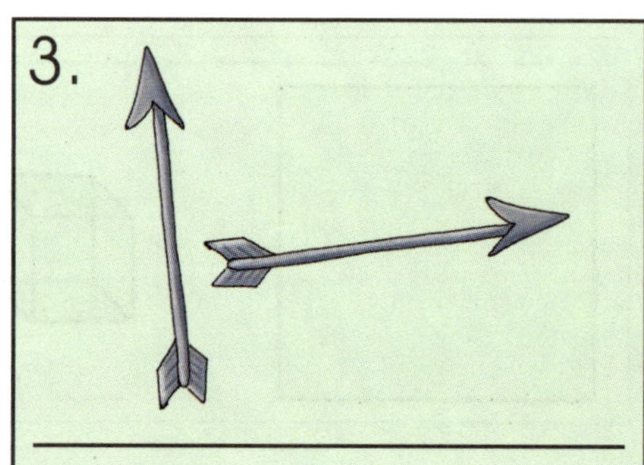

4.

5.

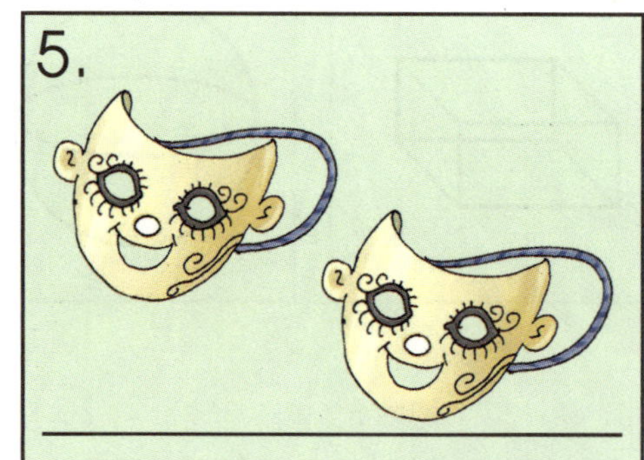

6.

TRY IT

Draw a letter to show flip and slide.

L

Flip, Turn and Slide

Draw a circle around the objects to show flip, slide and turn using the colour code.

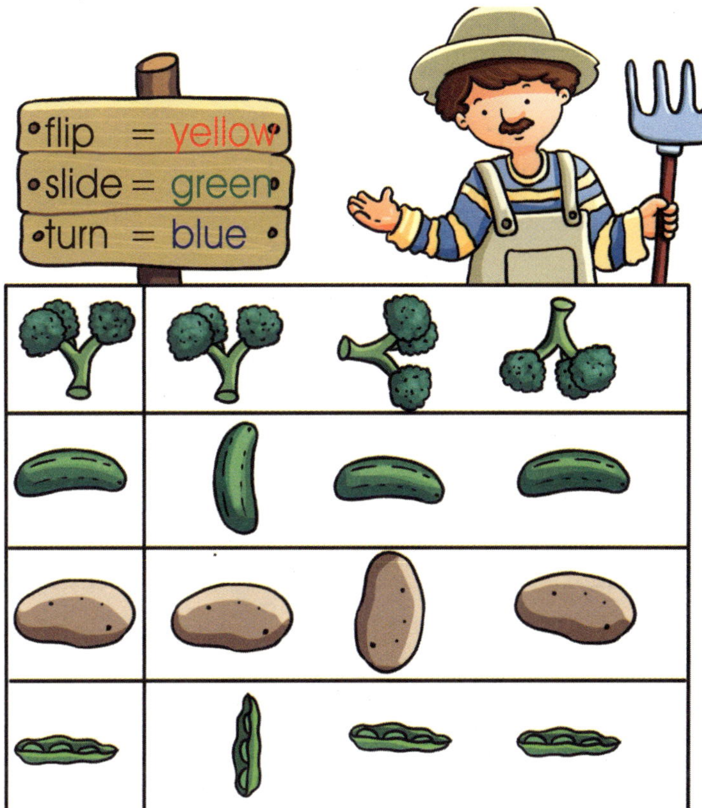

CHALLENGE

Draw a leaf. Then draw and label its flip, slide and turn.

Flip, Turn and Slide

Look at the figures below. Circle the one that is congruent to the first one in each row. Then label it as flip, slide or turn.

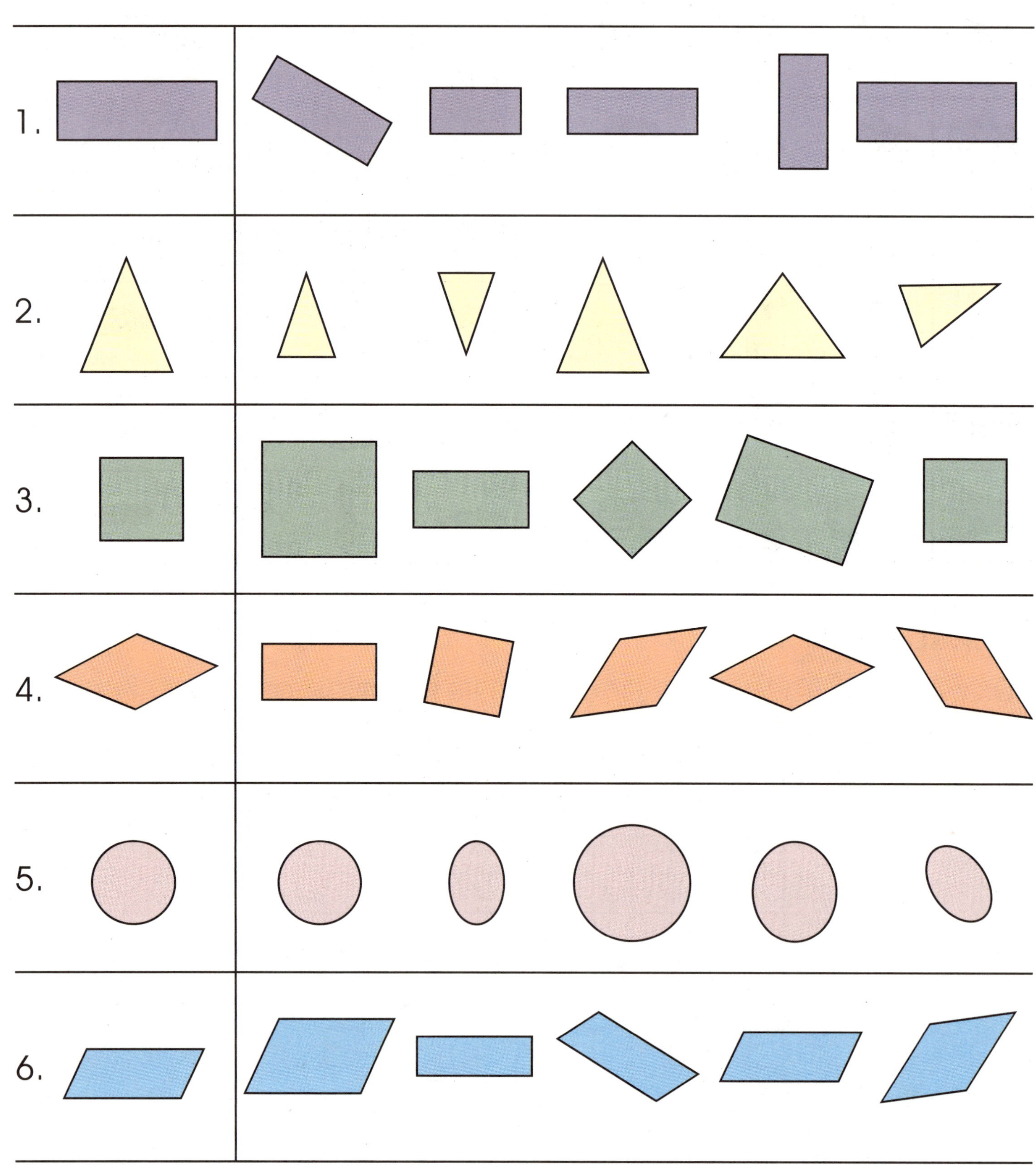

Equal Parts

Ronny has painted all the shapes. Draw a circle around the shapes that are divided into equal parts.

A shape can be divided into two, three, four or many equal parts.

Fractions

Look at the shapes. Each shape is divided into different number of equal parts.

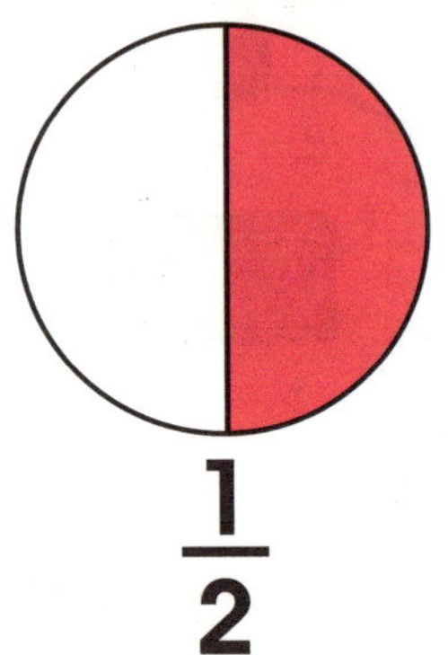

$\frac{1}{2}$

$\frac{1}{2}$ 1 ⟶ part coloured, 2 ⟶ number of equal parts

$\frac{1}{2}$ is a fraction. It is also called one-half.

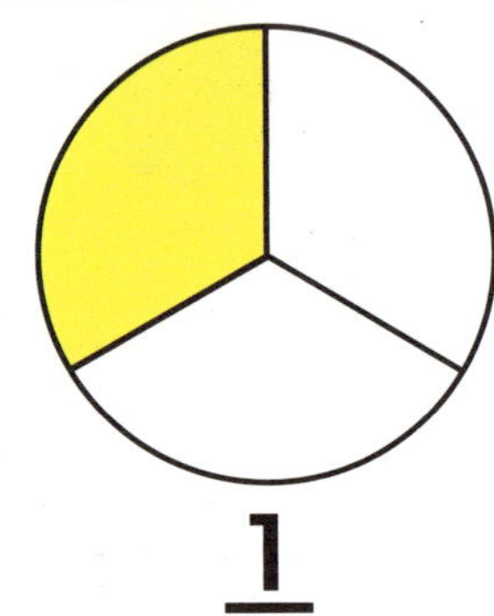

$\frac{1}{3}$

$\frac{1}{3}$ 1 ⟶ part coloured, 3 ⟶ number of equal parts

$\frac{1}{3}$ is a fraction. It is also called one-third.

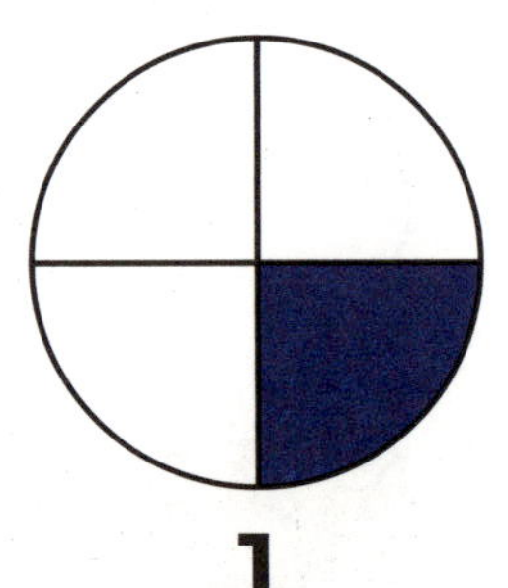

$\frac{1}{4}$

$\frac{1}{4}$ 1 ⟶ part coloured, 4 ⟶ number of equal parts

$\frac{1}{4}$ is a fraction. It is also called one-fourth or quarter.

A fraction also tells us that many parts of a whole are being used.

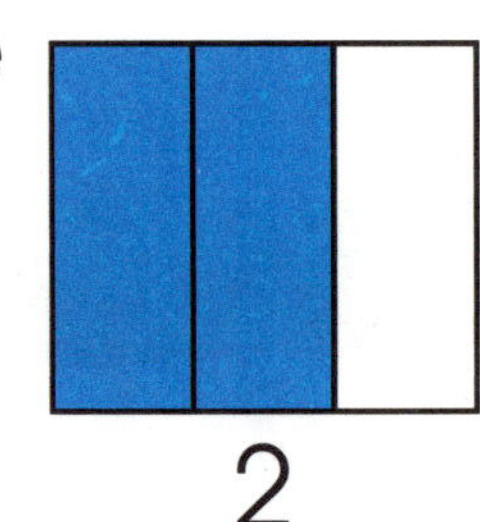

$\frac{2}{3}$

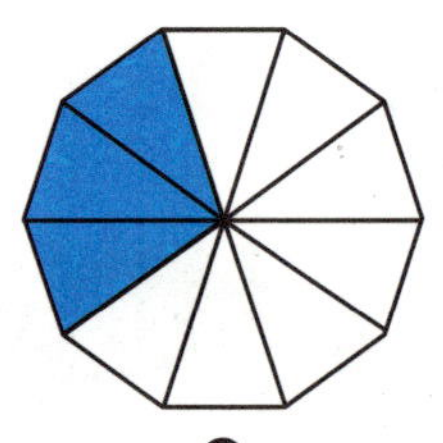

$\frac{3}{10}$

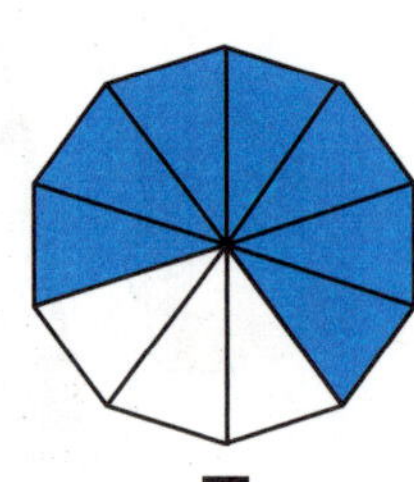

$\frac{7}{10}$

Fractions

Write the fraction for the shaded part.

Fractions

Shade each shape to show the fraction. Then write the fraction for the unshaded part.

A. shaded= $\frac{3}{4}$
unshaded=

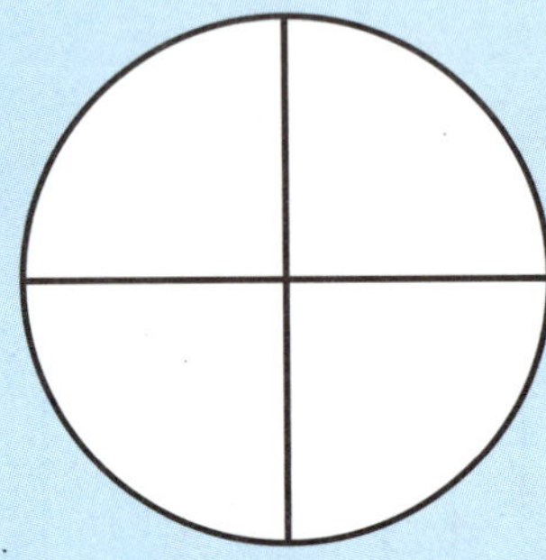

B. shaded= $\frac{1}{2}$
unshaded=

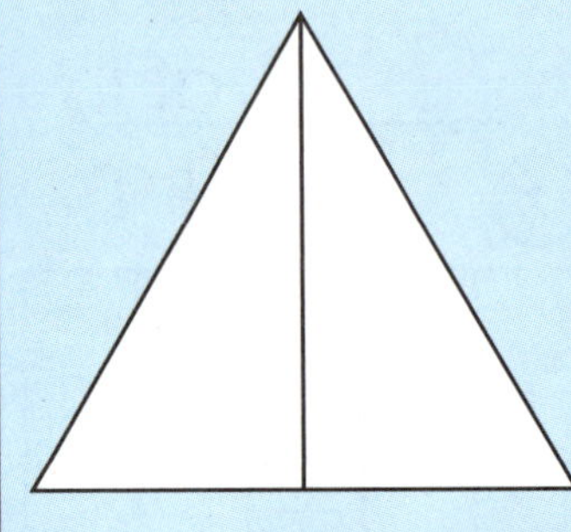

C. shaded= $\frac{2}{4}$
unshaded=

D. shaded= $\frac{5}{6}$
unshaded=

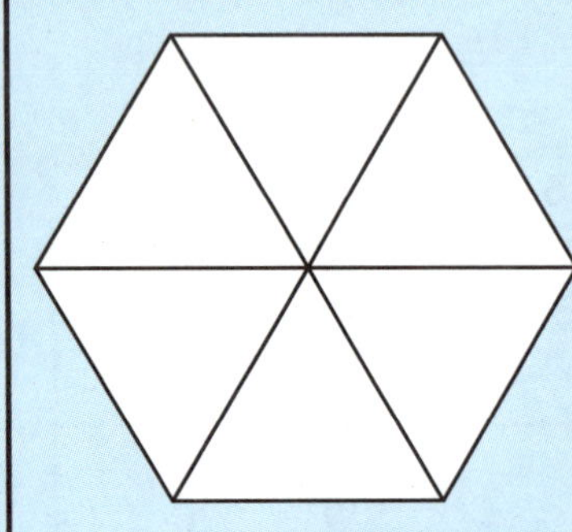

E. shaded= $\frac{2}{3}$
unshaded=

F. shaded= $\frac{3}{10}$
unshaded=

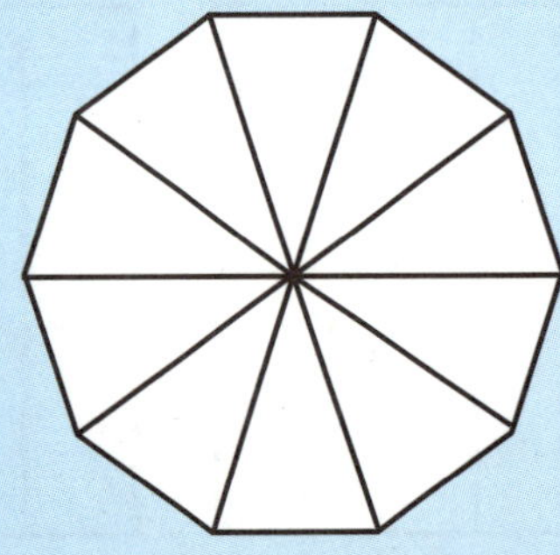

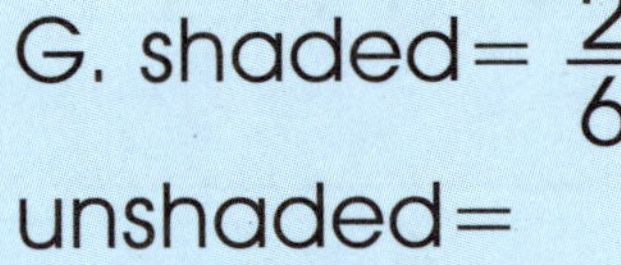

G. shaded= $\frac{2}{6}$
unshaded=

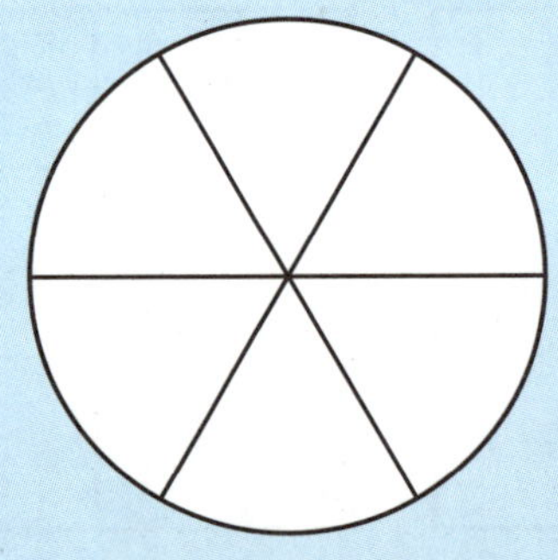

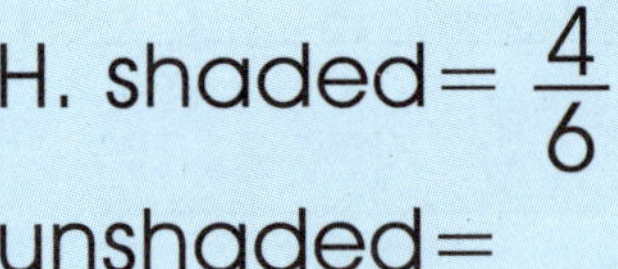

H. shaded= $\frac{4}{6}$
unshaded=

I. shaded= $\frac{7}{8}$
unshaded=

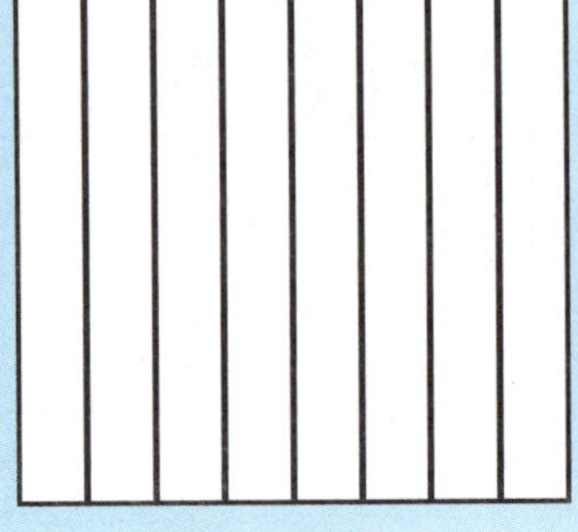

J. shaded= $\frac{1}{4}$
unshaded=

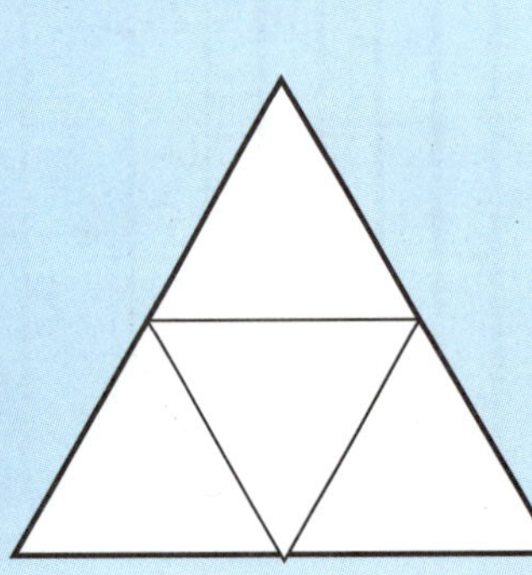

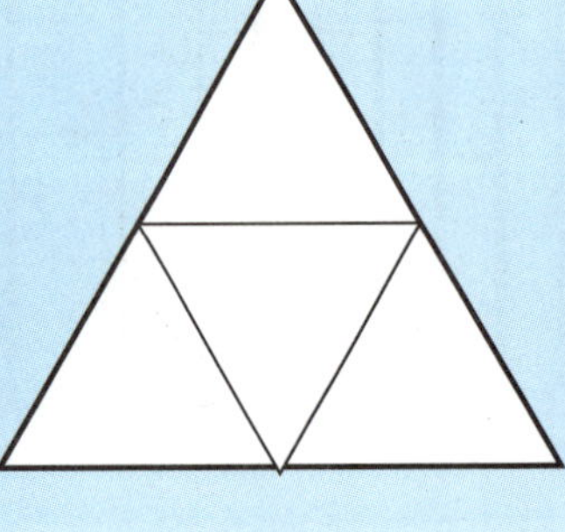

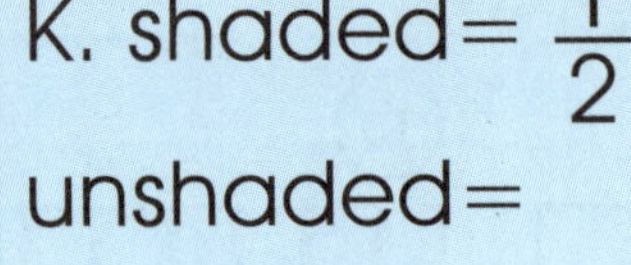

K. shaded= $\frac{1}{2}$
unshaded=

L. shaded= $\frac{4}{8}$
unshaded=

Telling Time to the Hour and Half Hour

Look at the small hand. The number it points is the hour. Look at the big hand. If it is at 12, write **o'clock**.

Look at the last number the hour hand passed. Do not pass the hour hand. Look at the big hand. If it is at 6, write **30 minutes or half past**.

Write the time below each clock.

1

______

2

______

3
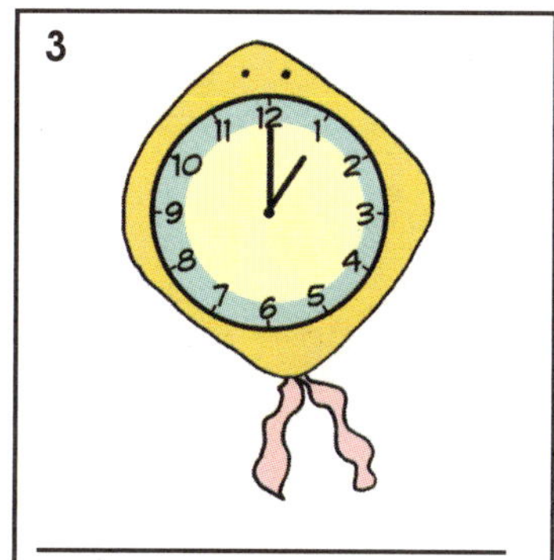
______

4
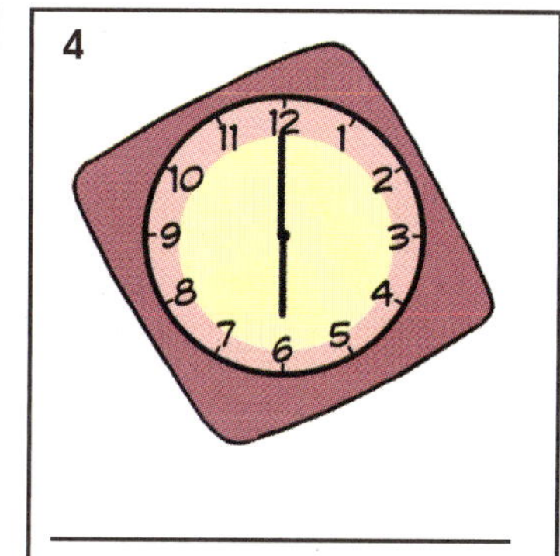
______

5

______

6

______

7
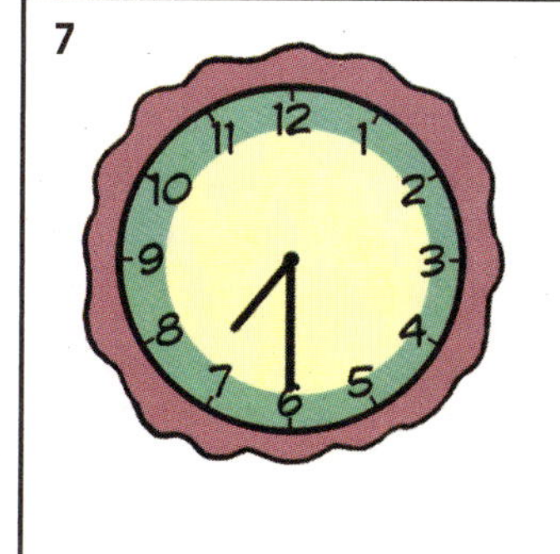
______

8
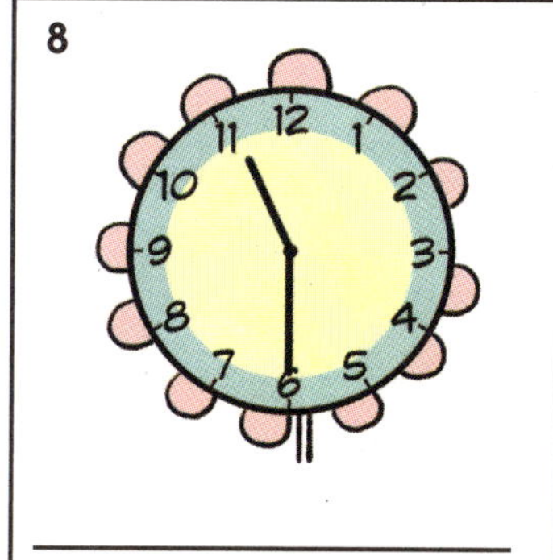
______

9

______

10
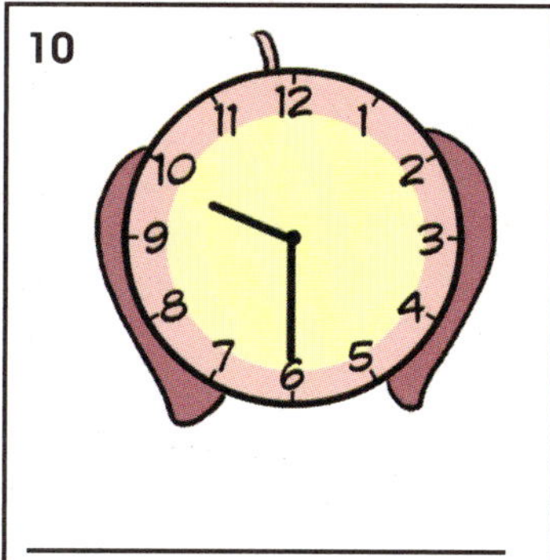
______

11
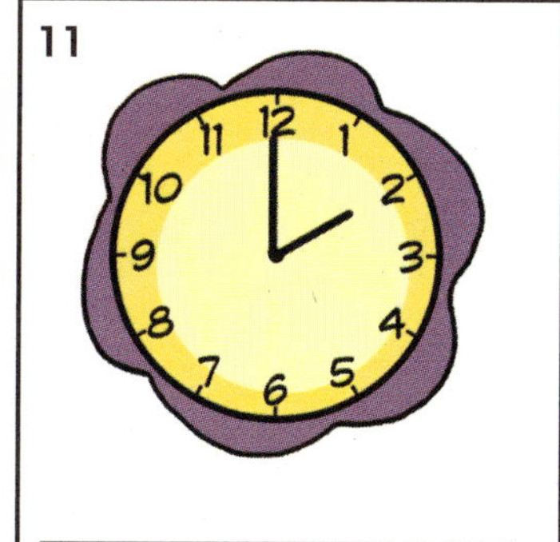
______

12
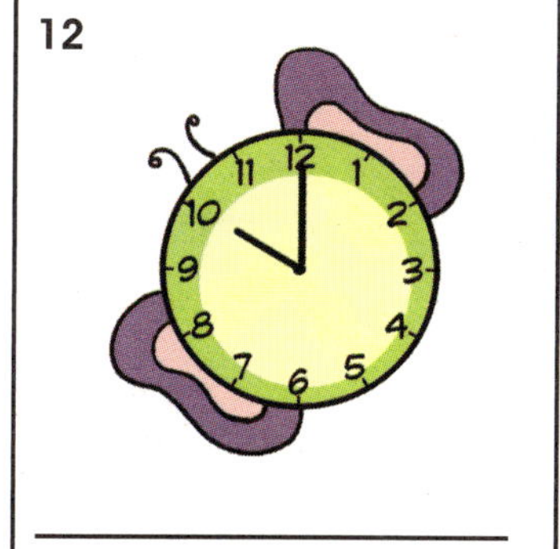
______

Telling Time to Quarter Hour

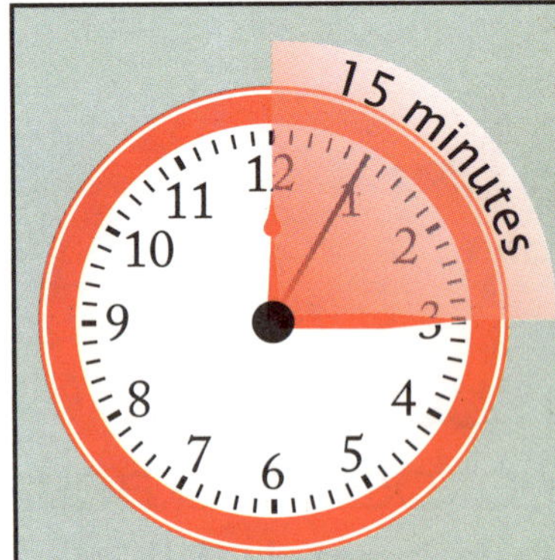

When the minute hand is at 3, we write **quarter past.**

When the minute hand is at 9, we write **quarter to.**

Write the time on the lines below each clock.

1 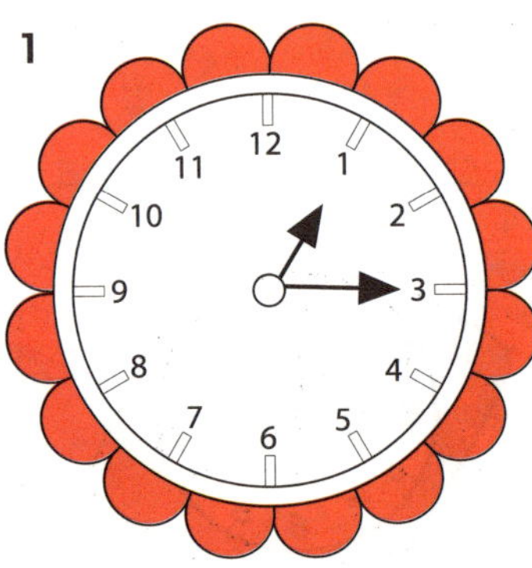

____

2 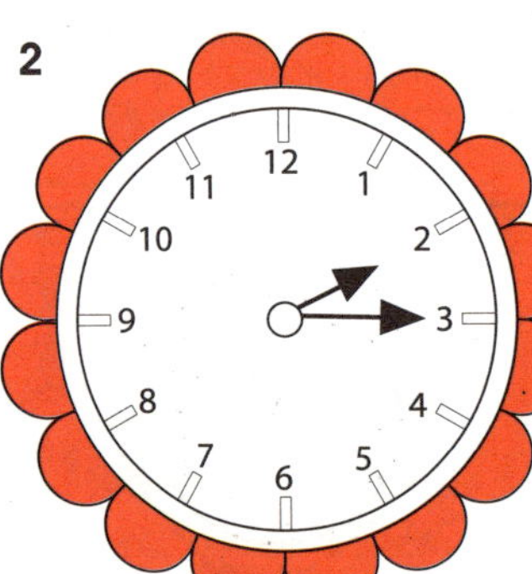

____

3 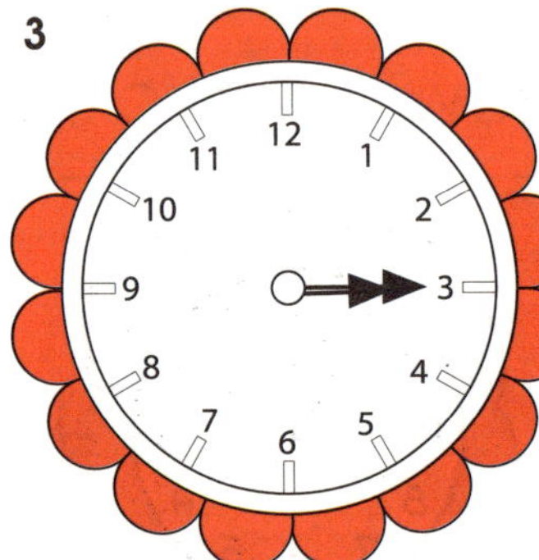

____

4 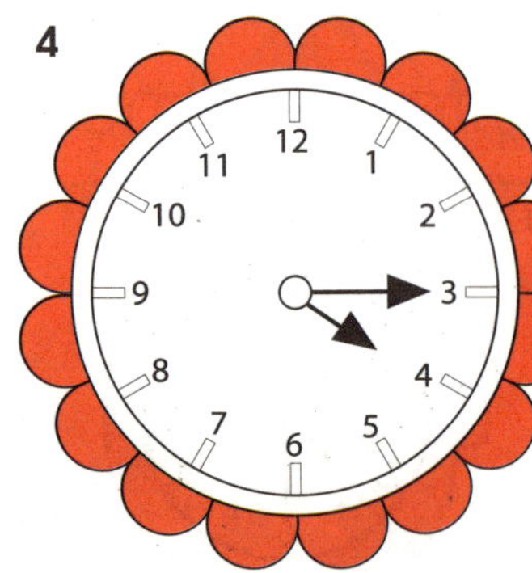

____

5 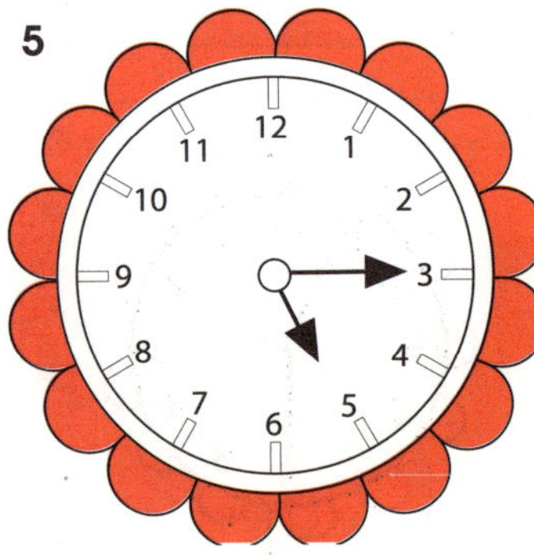

____

6 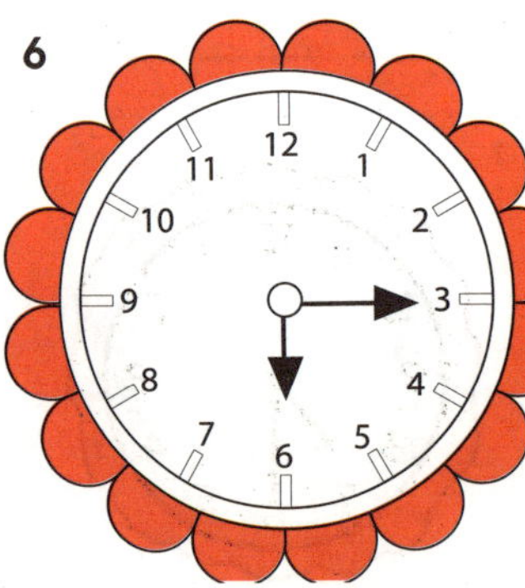

____

7 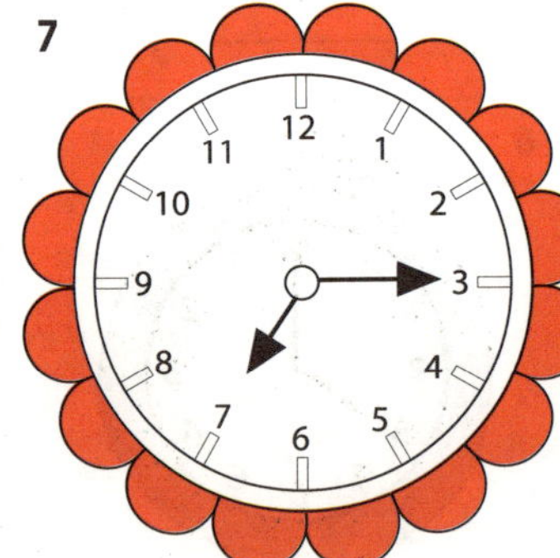

____

8 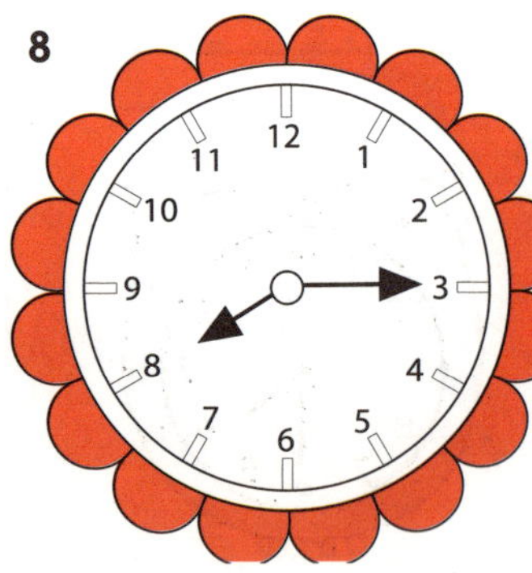

____

9 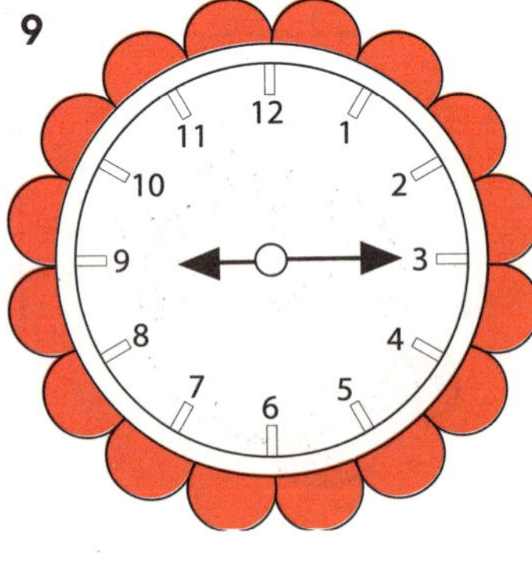

____

10 

____

11 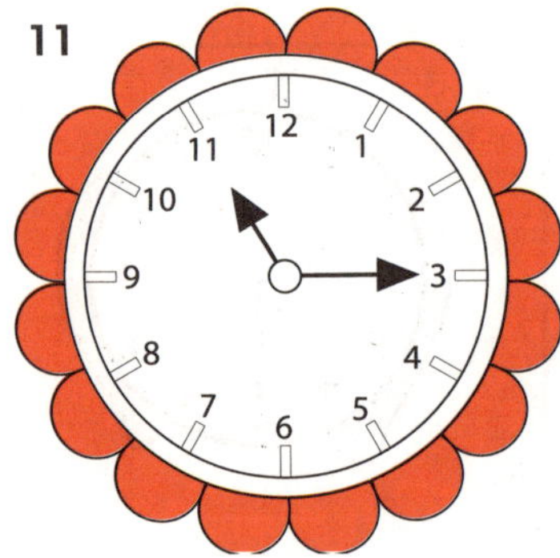

____

12 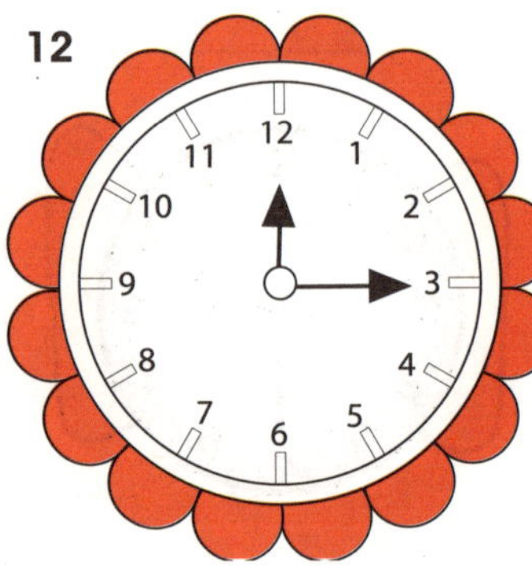

____

Telling Time

Identify the time on each clock. Then draw the symbol matching the correct clock.

☐ 3:00	☐ quarter to two
☐ 6:15	☐ half past five
☐ 2:45	☐ three o'clock
☐ 9:30	☐ quarter after twelve
☐ 5:30	☐ half past nine
☐ 11:15	☐ quarter after six
☐ 1:45	☐ quarter to three
☐ 12:15	☐ quarter after eleven

Telling Time to Minutes

What time is it? Draw the hands.

Look at the hour hand, what it's passed and STOP!

Look at the minute hand. Start at 12 and count by 5s!

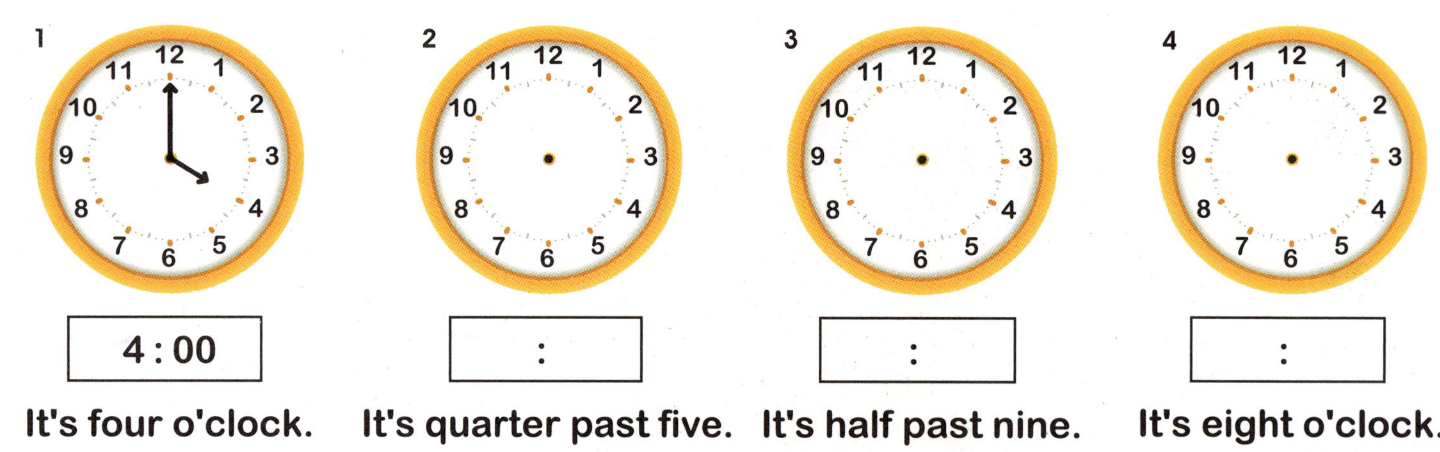

1 4 : 00 It's four o'clock.

2 : It's quarter past five.

3 : It's half past nine.

4 : It's eight o'clock.

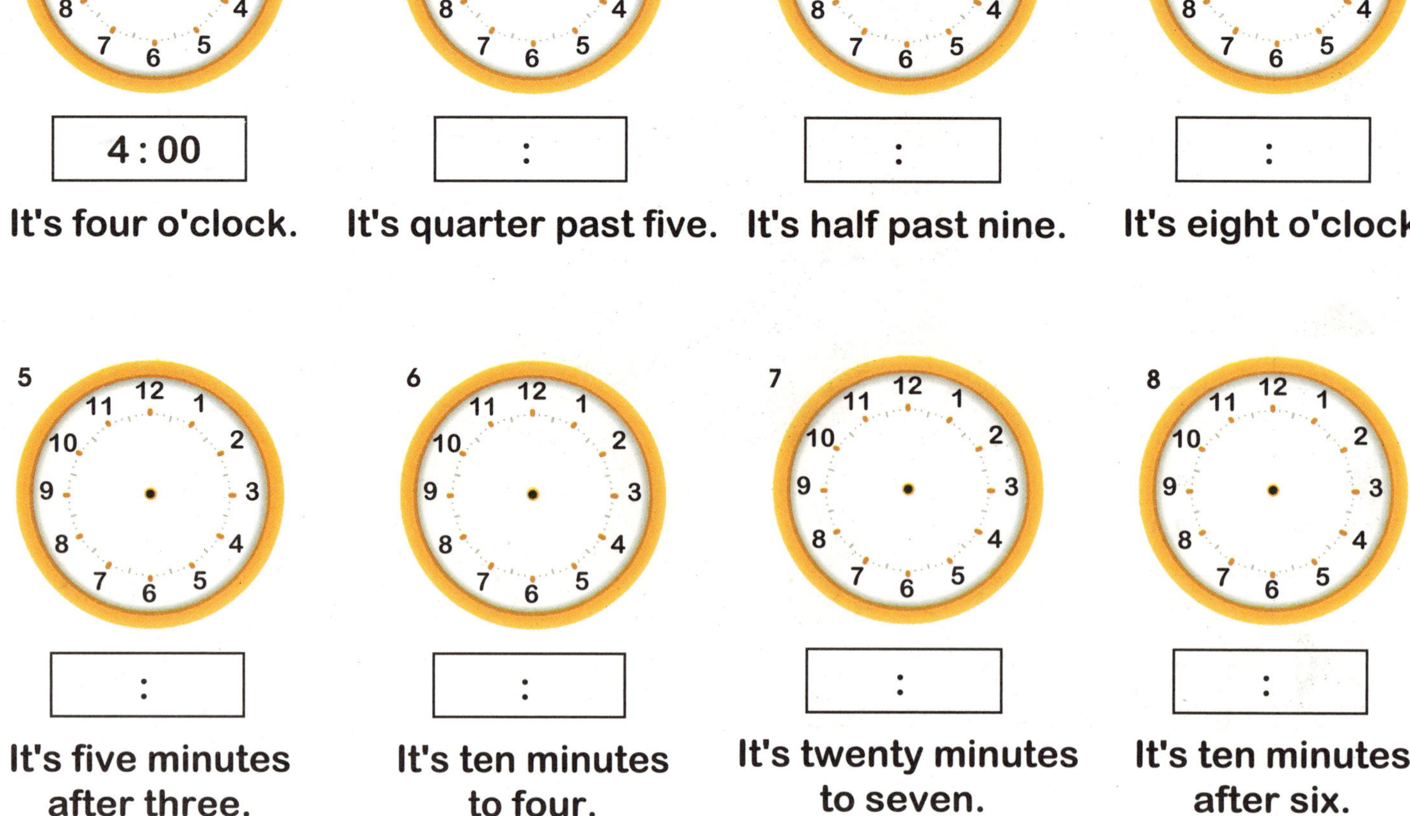

5 : It's five minutes after three.

6 : It's ten minutes to four.

7 : It's twenty minutes to seven.

8 : It's ten minutes after six.

Measuring Length in Centimetres

Length is how long or far something is. We measure length in centimetres, inches or metres.

cm= centimetres, in= inches, m= metres

centimetre
The length of a paper clip

inch
The length of a pinky finger

metres
a bit more than width of a door

Look at each fence. Guess the length and then use a ruler to measure actually.

guess = _____ cm

actual measure = _____ cm

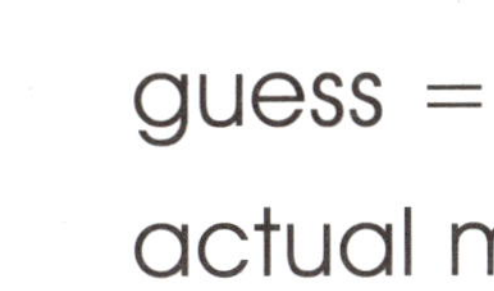

guess = _____ cm

actual measure = _____ cm

guess = _____ cm

actual measure = _____ cm

guess = _____ cm

actual measure = _____ cm

guess = _____ cm

actual measure = _____ cm

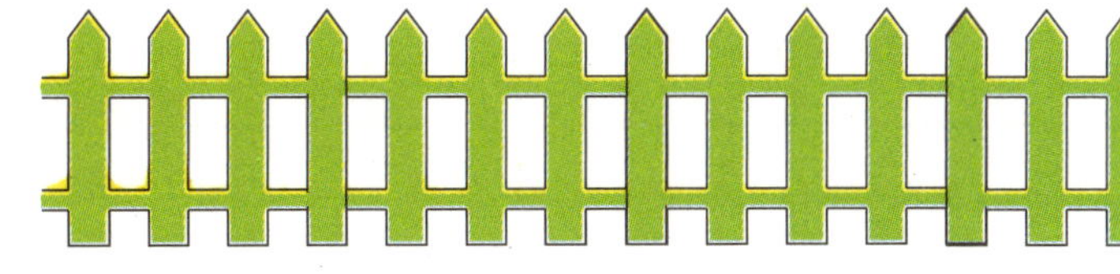

guess = _____ cm

actual measure = _____ cm

CHALLENGE

Draw a fence that is longer than the longest fence on this page.

Measuring Length in Centimetres

Use a ruler to measure these lines in centimetres. Then add all the measurements and write the total.

Total length= ______ cm

Total length= ______ cm

Total length= ______ cm

Guess the length of each object in centimetres. Then measure to find the length.

Objects to measure	My guess	Actual measurement	Colour a star for each correct guess
My hand	______ cm	______ cm	☆
My book	______ cm	______ cm	☆
A pencil	______ cm	______ cm	☆
My foot	______ cm	______ cm	☆

Measuring Length in Inches

How long are these things? Measure in inches and write.

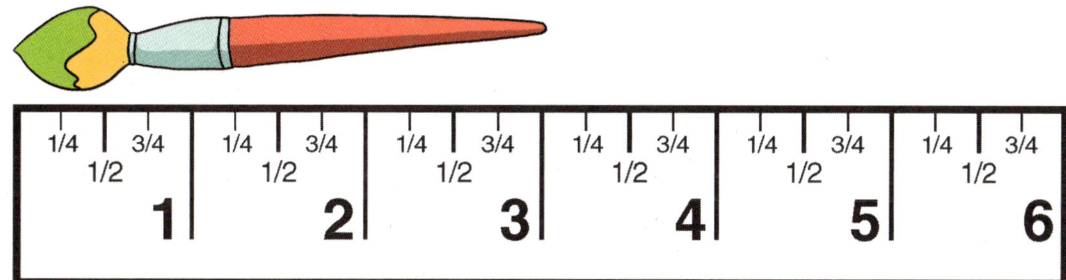

____

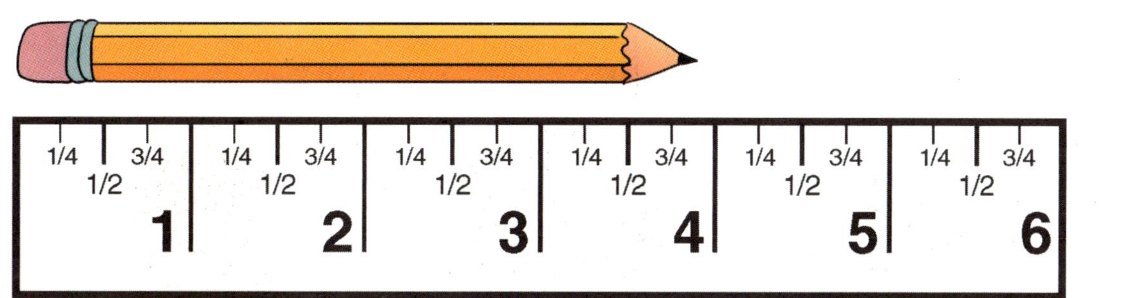

____

Guess the length of each object in inches. Then measure to find the length.

Objects to measure	My guess	Actual measurement	Colour a star for each correct guess
My hand	________ in	________ in	☆
My book	________ in	________ in	☆
A pencil	________ in	________ in	☆
My foot	________ in	________ in	☆

CHALLENGE

How could you measure the length of this line?

How long is it?

Weight

Weight is how heavy or light something is. We measure weight in grams and kilograms.

kg= kilograms   g= grams

Envelope **measured in Grams**

Rock **measured in kilograms**

Measure the weight of each object and write it below.

1 ________ kg

2 ________ g

3 ________ kg

4 ________ kg

5 ________ kg

6 ________ kg

7 ________ g

8 ________ kg

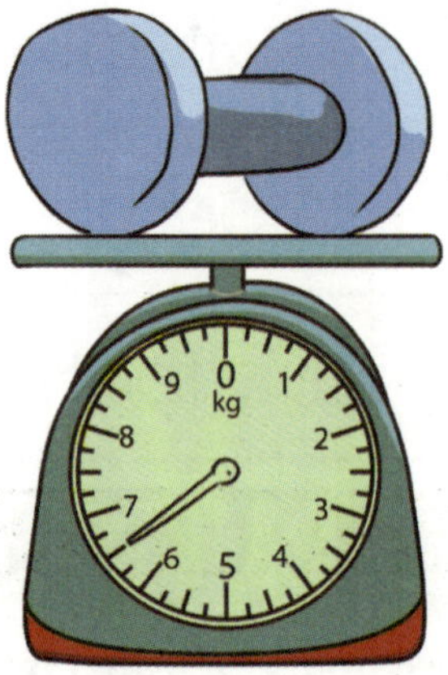

Weight

Draw a pointer on each scale to show the weight of each object below.

CHALLENGE

Can you find something that is of the same weight as you are.

Weight

Calculate the unknown weight to balance each scale.

Capacity

Capacity is how much liquid a container can hold. We measure capacity in litres and millilitres.

l= litres **ml= millilitres**

Glass of lemonade **measured in millilitres**

oil can **measured in litres**

These containers measure millilitres.

A.

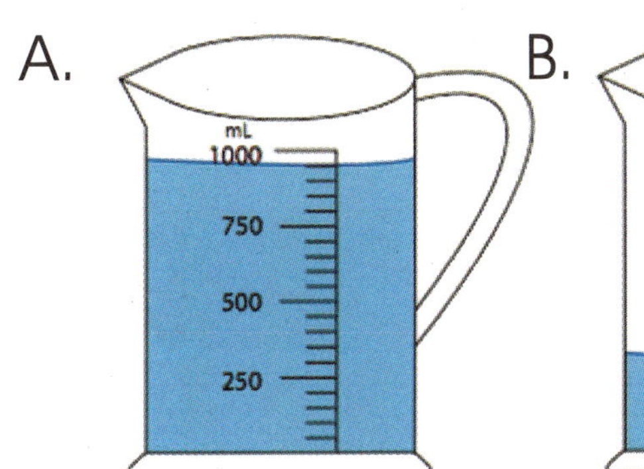

B. C.

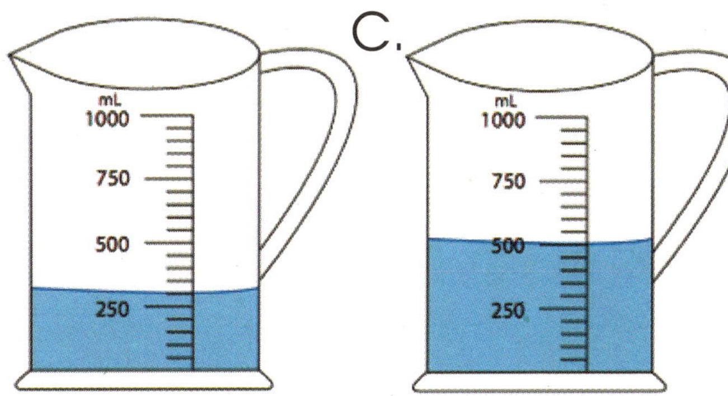

1. How much water is in:
   Container A: ________ Container B: ________
   Container C: ________
2. How much water is more in:
   C than B ? ________ A than C? ________ A than B? ________
3. Which container has water almost equal to 1L?

   ____

4. How much must be added to container C to make it 1 L?

   ____

CHALLENGE

Take a bottle and with a marker show where you think ½ L is. Measure and check.

Answer Key

Page 2

3 – rectangle	4 – square
5 – hexagon	6 – triangle
7 – rectangle	8 – octagon
9 – square	10 – pentagon

Page 3

Rectangle

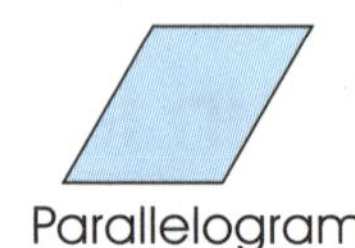

Parallelogram

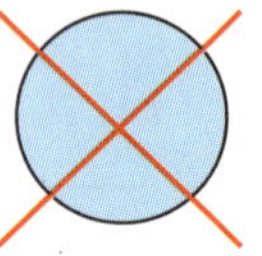

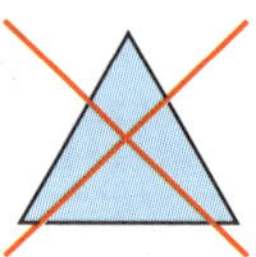

Square

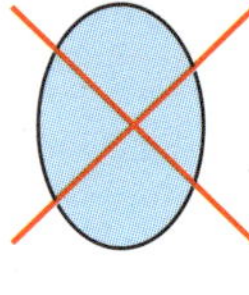

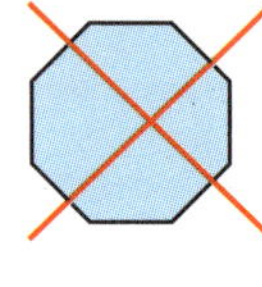

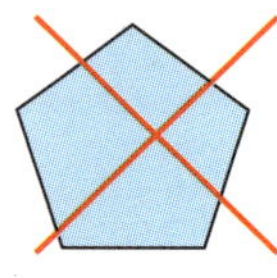

Page 4

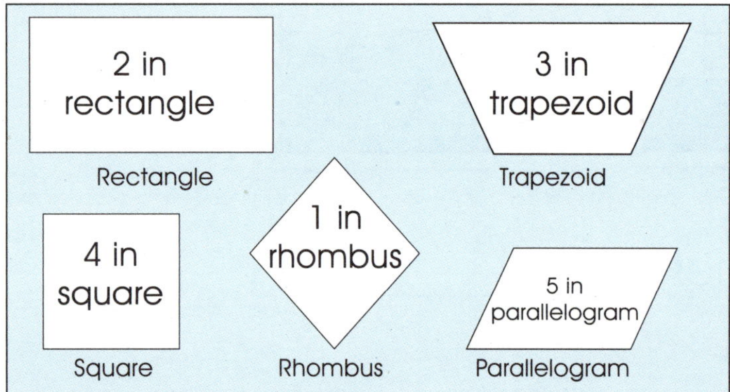

Page 5

1.  a. 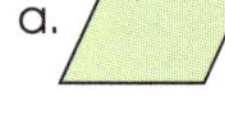 b. 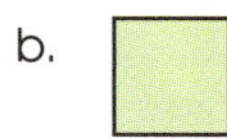  c. 

2.  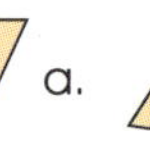 a.  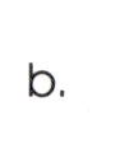 b. 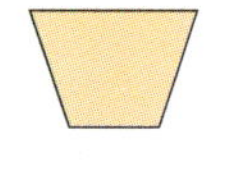 c. 

3.  a. 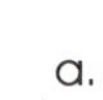 b. 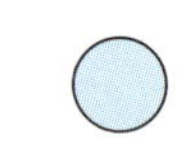  c.  

4.  a. 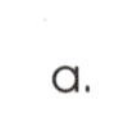 b.  c. 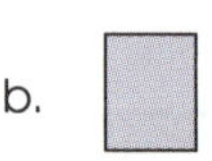 

5.  a. 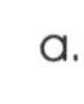 b.  c. 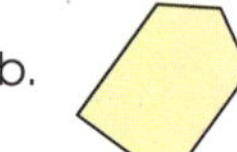 

Page 6

1. E	2. O
3. A	4. NONE
5. I AND M	6. H
7. G	8. B
9. NONE	10. C
11. F	12. R

Page 7

Children will draw shapes on their own.

Page 8

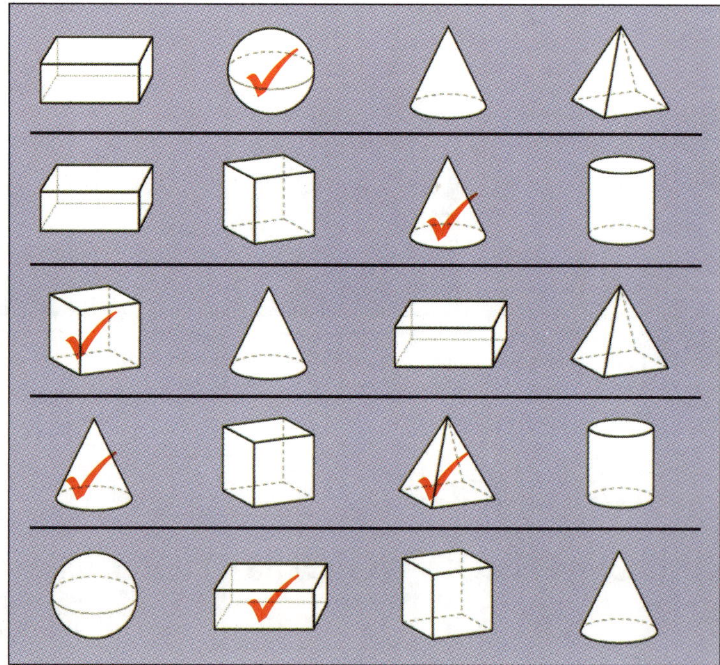

Page 9

Children will do on their own.

Page 10

1. 6
2. 5 (write 2 under triangle and 3 under rectangle)
3. 6 (write 6 under square)
4. 6 (write 2 under square and 4 under rectangle)

Answer Key

Page 11

Children will do on their own.

Page 12

1. Flip
2. Slide
3. Turn
4. Turn
5. Slide
6. Flip

Page 13

Children will do on their own.

Page 14

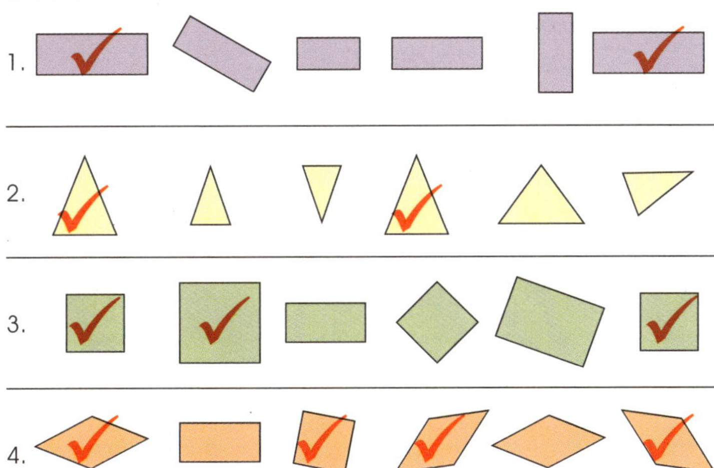

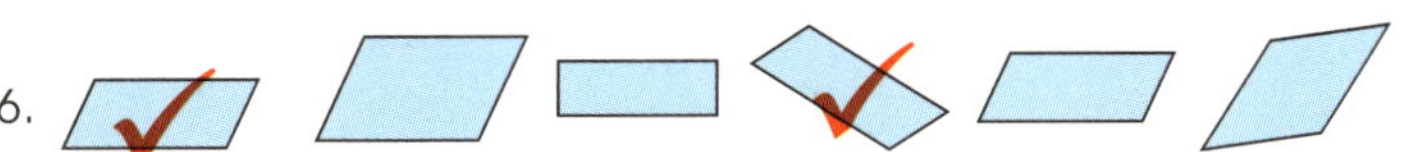

Page 15

Page 17

1. 1, 2. 1/2, 3. 1/3, 4. 1/4,
5. 6/8, 6. 6/9, 7. 8/10, 8. 7/9,
9. 3/5, 10. 4/6, 11. 4/7, 12. 4/12,
13. 5/13, 14. 10/14

Page 18

Children will do it on their own.

Page 19

1. 7:30, 2. 11:00, 3. 1:00, 4. 6:00,
5. 4:30, 6. 8:00, 7. 7:30, 8. 11:30,
9. 2:30, 10. 9:30, 11. 2:00, 12. 10:00

Page 20

1. 1:15, 2. 2:15, 3. 3:15, 4. 4:15,
5. 5:15, 6. 6:15, 7. 7:15, 8. 8:15,
9. 9:15, 10. 10:15, 11. 11:15, 12. 12:15

Answer Key

Page 21
Children will draw shapes on their own.

Page 22
Children will draw shapes on their own.

Page 23
Children will draw shapes on their own.

Page 24
Children will draw shapes on their own.

Page 25
The length of paint brush is 3 inches.

The length of the pencil is 3 ¾ inches.

Page 26
1. 3.5kg, 2. 750g, 3. 5.5kg, 4. 1.5kg,
5. 3.8kg, 6. 2.3kg, 7. 750kg, 8. 6.5kg

Page 27
Children will draw shapes on their own

Page 28
3 kg, 1kg

4 kg, 100g

50g, 3kg

5 kg, 100g

Page 29
1. 900 ml, 260 ml, 500 ml
2. 240 ml, 400 ml, 650 ml
3. Container A
4. 500 ml